JA WELL NO, FINE

AN ALTERNATIVE GUIDE TO SOUTH AFRICA

TIM RICHMAN
&
STUART HENDRICKS

A **Aaaargh!** African handshakes, fist bum[p]
(v Western time) The ANC **The Arms Deal** **B**
Born-frees Braais **The bush** **C** **Cape Town** Ca[
Sunday night Loser's Complex **The Constituti[on**
Driving **Durban** "Dwaal" **E** **EFF** "Eish" **English** [
Finding coconuts **The fracking Karoo** Fynbos **G**[
"Gogga" **The great emigration debate** **H** "H[
Cape storms **(v KZN tornados)** Hipsters **The** [
su-u-u-gaaar" Indians **isiLanguage confus[ion**
Johannesburg, as a world-class African city [
The leaf-blower problem **Lowveld sunsets** Th[e
Madonsela Mielies **Minibus taxis** "Mlungu" "[
national bird of South Africa The NEC of th[e
O **Okes, chinas & boytjies** Other cities in [
attendants Political *Come on-s!* **Poolitics** Pron[
Cyril Ramaphosa **Robot hawkers** The rooi g[
Strike season Supermarkets **The swart gev[aar**
Tripartite Alliance **Two-tone shirts** **U** **The (un[**
struggle songs Unimpeachable legends of Sout[h
W **Weather misconceptions** "Wena?" / "Jy?" [
Y "Yebo"/ "Ja"/ "Ewe" Youth unemployability "[

nd all-round greeting madness **Africa time**

alas" Bergies **Biltong** Boerewors v braai wors

rds **Cars & cellphones** *Carte Blanche*-induced

me & corruption **D Nkosazana Dlamini-Zuma**

s teams The evolution of kwaito **F Fast food**

artjies Game rangers **"Give that man a Bell's"**

g a cadenza" "Hayibo!" **Highveld storms v**

ne Affairs revolution "Howzit" **I "I lo-o-o-ve**

J "Ja well no fine" Jews **Johannesburg**

Kak" "Kiff" **KZN power L Laager mentality**

inescent rise of SA's black diamonds **M Thuli**

, **donner, bliksem"** Aaron Motsoaledi **N The**

IC **Nkandla** "Now", "now now" & "just now"

Orlando **Pirates v Kaizer Chiefs P Petrol**

Protea problems **Q Queuing R The race card**

S Shark-cage diving Springbok madness

"T.I.A." The tokoloshe **Township tours** The

dably confrontational) **misinterpretation of**

a **The unlawful police V "Voetsek!"** Vuvuzelas

your bru, bro? **X Lulu Xingwana** Xylophones

s & jislaaik" **Z Zapiro** Helen Zille **Jacob Zuma**

Published by Two Dogs
an imprint of Burnet Media

•

Burnet Media is the publisher of Mercury and Two Dogs books
PO Box 53557, Kenilworth, 7745
South Africa

info@burnetmedia.co.za
www.burnetmedia.co.za
Twitter: @TwoDogs_Mercury
Facebook: Two Dogs / Mercury

•

First published 2013
1 3 5 7 9 8 6 4 2

•

Distributed by Jacana Media www.jacana.co.za
Printed and bound by Ultra Litho, Johannesburg

•

ISBN 9780987043740

Burnet Media |

About the authors

Tim Richman and **Stuart Hendricks** are part of the South African book industry. They have participated – in authoring, editing, publishing and/or general handlanging capacities – in the creation of more than 40 titles, including the bestselling *Is It Just Me Or Is Everything Kak?* series.

Acknowledgments

From Tim: Many thanks to those who contributed to the book, including Francesca Bourke; Dylan Muhlenberg and Tudor Caradoc-Davies; Stephen Grootes; Azad Essa; Geoff and Nikki Chennels; Tricia Rowand; Bob Rowand; Sharon Boonzaier and Simon Richman; Rupert Butler; Guy Dviri; Steve Loubser; Jon & Nikki Burnett, Michelle Erasmus, Edward Durrant, Natasha Kypriotis; Vito da Silva; Mark During, Chris Warncke and Oliver Genthe; Greg Boyes; Ace, Robbie B, Brad, Bretto, Finch, Larry, Pom, Ceddie, Paulie, Mike R and the rest of the 4T group (not a cycling group); as usual, SASASU (not a trade union); and, most of all, to Jules.

From Stuart: Thanks go to Robert, Felicia and Alastair Hendricks, and the Hendricks clan at large; Sven Adams; the Greensiders of '07; the FST; Claremont Corps; the Bay Harbitrarians; and, finally, to Nabila Jossie, whose incisive observations keep me sane – thank you for your selflessness, encouragement and love.

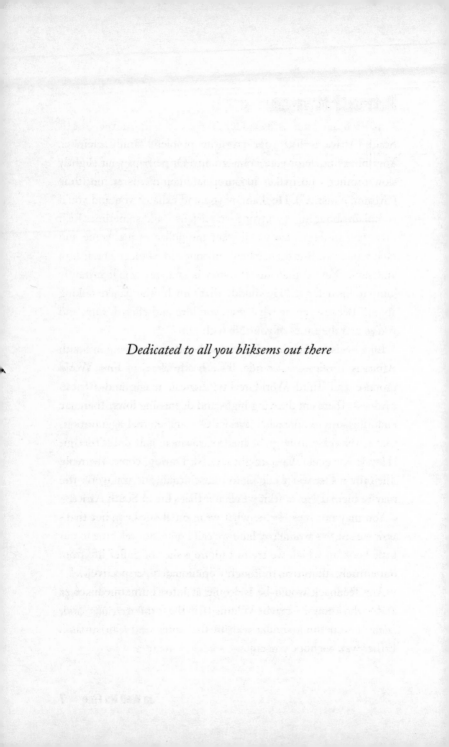

Dedicated to all you bliksems out there

Introduction

South Africa is like your favourite problem family member. Your boozy uncle or your crazy granny. Or perhaps your slightly slow brother who makes inappropriate comments at mealtime ("Mmm, moist…"). He'll annoy you and exhaust you and you'll complain about him to anyone who listens – and sometimes he'll drive you so demented you'll want the police to just come and take him away. But then, when someone else is mean about him and says, "Yussis, that guy Royston is strange", you'll instantly jump to his defence. "Hey buddy, that's my brother you're talking about!" Because, come what may, you love and cherish him, and you've had the times of your life with him.

Like a Sunday lunch with your brother Royston, living in South Africa is a roller-coaster ride. It's a heady blend of First World promise and Third World reality; African magic and African madness. There are dizzying highs and depressing lows. There are enduring joys to appreciate every day – and eternal aggravations that never cease. Life grabs hold of you here and doesn't let go. "Hey, let me go, life," you might say. "No, I won't," comes the reply. Then you realise you're talking to yourself again and you worry you may be bipolar. Never fear; we all are. That's life in South Africa.

You may not have a clue what we're on about here, but that's how we see this wonderful land we call home. So welcome to our little book, in which we try to capture a slice of Saffer life from our entirely subjective, thoroughly opinionated perspective.

Any feedback would be welcome at info@burnetmedia.co.za and – who knows? – maybe Volume II, in the form of *Ag No Shame Man* or something similar will hit the stores next Christmas… Either way, we hope you enjoy.

Aaaargh!
(with a bit of Affirmative Action)

politics / cliché

A-Z collections are very handy in that, well, they're set out from A to Z. In terms of the order of things, there appear to be no agendas and there's no worrying about who comes first – which in South Africa can be a problem. You could, of course, change **Kwaito** to **The evolution of kwaito** if you've got too many Ks, and you could put an **Unlawful** in front of **Police** if you needed another U, but mostly it sorts itself out. Problem is we don't want to start with AA, do we? Because Affirmative Action is just so tired and boring and either you believe in it or you don't or you believe the theory but not the practice. Yawn. And of course there's no way you can start with AA and write about Alcoholics Anonymous or the Automobile Association because AA in South Africa means bloody Affirmative Action, and it very quickly leads to its cousin BEE, Black Economic Empowerment...

So what, aardvarks? Aardwolfs? Aasvoëls? This isn't an animal encyclopaedia, people, it's an alternative guide to South Africa. It would've been nice to start with Aaron Motsoaledi because then we could kick things off on a positive note, but we're alphabetising by surname unfortunately, which means you'll find him under M and bang goes that idea.

So we're going with **Aaaargh!** Use it as a daily mantra when you read the newspaper headlines. Or as your response to another AA/BEE conversation.

African handshakes, fist bumps and all-round greeting madness behaviour / greetings

South Africa is a place with 11 official languages and a thousand unofficial handshakes. Whether it's the finger-snapper or the thumb-bending-knuckle-bump-palm-pistol, meeting someone requires translating a five-fingered Tower of Babel if you have the vaguest intention of getting it right.

The obvious puzzler is what we'll call, for want of a better term, the "African handshake". That's where you start with a firm handclasp, swap once to an inverted handclasp, and revert back to the initial handclasp. You know, so that the grasp is effortlessly changed midway by both parties, but quickly and smoothly... Still not with me? Okay, slowly this time: it's a three-stage process of grip, swing palm around thumb area and grip again. Seeing as I've explained it three times now you should be able to pull one off, but then, given our endless cultural misunderstandings and misconceptions, unless you've danced a mile in someone else's gumboots it's even more difficult knowing when it's okay to use it. Especially if you've been born with the racial handicap of being white. Will you come across as patronising if you do it and the other (NB: black!) person doesn't? And if you don't do it, and they do, will you look like a honky for not being down?

Then there's the Indian whose grip is softer than a baby's thighs, and his physical opposite, the Afrikaner, who politely and reverently crushes every bone in your hand to dust with his ham-sized bear paw. Worse still is the modern barrage of newfangled new-tribe greetings – complex hand-dances with thumb pushes and slaps and twists and an interval at half-time and maybe a shoulder nudge to conclude. Try meeting one of these concoctions with a standard, firm handshake and *you're* the one who looks lame, not the tattooed douchebag in the Tapout vest and bedazzled Ed Hardy jeans.

Next up is the fist bump, which is great in that you're not inviting whatever the other guy has been handling to contaminate your open palm. What isn't so great is when you go in for a bump but the guy's waiting there with a regular handshake and so you turn your rock to paper just in time to meet his rock... Or when neither of you alter your shake style and so you end up grabbing hold of his fist and kind of pulling on it like a one-armed bandit. Or sometimes you'll get a guy who fist bumps and then opens his hand as though it's exploding in slow motion and, while looking at it, he actually says, "Boom". Honestly, what the f–?

What else? Those hug and pound African-American things, like, yo-bro-I-saw-this-on-Channel-O-once-so-now-I'm-gonna-do-this-racially-charged-fist-bump-hug-thing too! Don't. After all, the whole point of a handshake is to keep your dick at arm's-length from the other guy's (isn't it?), so why would you go against all that is good and touch crotches? High-fives?

Absolutely fine. Until someone goes high when you're low, or low and you're holding it up high or, worse still, leaves you hanging – the ultimate social rejection. Then you get the guy who, because you high-fived him once at the beginning of the evening, feels it's open season and wants to slap palms with you at every punchline, every round of drinks, every time a pretty girl walks by... Am I right or am I right!? *high-fives*

What we need is some formal etiquette to stop the uncoordinated, socially dispiriting, frankly ridiculous handshake action going on out there. Someone needs to assume the leadership role and signal clearly and with conviction as to the handshaking or fist-bumping or high-fiving or pounding-and-hugging or palm-tickling that is about to take place. Better yet, can we simply agree to greet with the common or garden, middle-of-the-road, grown-ass man handshake? That's the straightforward lining up and then clasping of right hands, two pumps and release. Not too hard, not too soft, just right. Baby bear stuff. When we depart we can do it again. No dead-fish limpwrister or machismo-laden handcrusher.

Other rules. Unless you're a used-car salesman you should never hold on for longer than a single "One Mississippi". And unless you're actually in politics, the politician's handshake – that move where you double-team the other person's hand with both of yours – is totally off limits and you may well be punched in the face.

Greeting a person who isn't a man? Do yourself a favour and just run away. Rather go and become a hermit somewhere quiet and speak to squirrels instead of manoeuvring yourself around this mess. Handshake? Kiss? Air kiss, kiss on one cheek, two cheeks, three cheeks, four cheeks (!), lips (!!), light hug, normal hug, hug-squeeze, awkward breast encounter with your aunt Wendy...?

Western time is a metronome. It is objective, something that exists independent of man. There are weeks in a year, days in a week, hours in a day, minutes in an hour, seconds in a minute. By delineating the universe in this fashion, the future can be accurately planned. Arrangements can be made. Things can get done in an efficient, sensible and predictable manner.

Africa time does not follow this logic. Africa time is elastic and subjective; it comes and it goes. Like the sound of a tree falling in the woods, it only happens if someone is around to experience it happening.

Well, that's the theory anyway, and if you want to explore it further, read the bit in *The Shadow Of The Sun* where Ryszard Kapuściński waits for a bus in Accra. Suffice to say, not many people operating on Africa time will have analysed it in as much detail as Kapuściński. They're too relaxed to bother. As a rule, people who operate on Africa time tend to have more chilled vibes and far lower blood pressure than people on Western time. (They also have less money.)

Here in South Africa, we experience both Western time and Africa time. It's part of our whole schizoid First World / Third World identity crisis. When we won the right to host the 2010 Soccer World Cup, it was on the understanding that, because people from around the world would be attending, it would be run according to Western time or else it wouldn't happen. New roads, major airport overhauls and world-class stadiums had to be completed by a certain date, and they were. (We rocked.) Our two massive new coal-fired power plants, on the other hand, are being built on Africa time. Both of them, Medupi in Limpopo and Kusile in Mpumalanga, were initially scheduled to start generating electricity in 2011, but they'll be done when they're done and it's a whole lot easier to simply accept that fact with a carefree shrug of the shoulders. Besides, when you're spending R240 billion, what's the rush?

Elsewhere, the Gautrain runs on Western time; minibus taxis do not. The surf scene chills on Africa time; cyclists live on Garmin-powered, satellite-guided, I-got-up-at-4.05am-to-ride-100-kilometres Western time. Home Affairs and your local traffic department swing from one to the other, depending on who the cabinet minister in charge is; and the advertising and design industries prefer Africa time, but finance and investment don't.

In social terms, Johannesburg generally runs on Western time, because it's the financial powerhouse of the country (and remember: if you're not on time you're losing money and what the hell's the matter with you?). As a result, it's considered poor form to arrive for a 7pm dinner party in, say, Parktown North later than 7.10pm. In fact, you can expect the average Parktown North dinner guest to arrive bang on time, and if someone isn't there by half past the hour then he's probably been hijacked.

In Cape Town it's downright rude to arrive at 7pm. *What the hell, man? You see how I'm in my towel and my hair's wet? That's because I had to get out of the shower to let you in.* This is because in Cape Town a stated 7pm start time is merely a guide as to the time at which you should mentally start preparing yourself to go out. Anyone who arrives at 7.15pm is technically early, and your host is really expecting you between 7.30ish and 8pm, or thereabouts. He's also expecting at least one guest to arrive two-and-a-half hours late with the excuse, *Sorry bru, I lost track of the time.*

That all said, no-one has dinner in Cape Town at 7pm. What planet are you on?

The ANC

The African National Congress is, as they say, a broad church. It has been and is many different things to many different people, both within and outside the party.

The apartheid government thought the ANC a motley collection of heathen commie terrorists.

Nelson Mandela described the ANC at the Rivonia Trial in 1964 as the party "that stood for a non-racial democracy" and "the concept of freedom and fulfilment for the African people in their own land".

British journalist Jason Cowley, writing in the *New Statesman* in 1999, labelled the modern ANC "an elected dictatorship".

According to Jacob Zuma, talking in 1996, the ANC is "more important" than the Constitution and, this time in 2008, is "even blessed in Heaven [which is why it] will rule until Jesus comes back".

For tweeters using the hashtag #BroughtToYouByANC, the ANC is evidently the cause of all the world's problems.

To the (huge) majority that keep it in power, the ANC is the party for the people, the emancipators who delivered democracy, freed the country and improved the lives of millions.

To the (increasingly mobilised) minority that oppose it, the ANC is a liberation movement that never worked out how to become a governing party.

Then there's Thought Leader blogger Manqoba Nxumalo's take on it. For him, the ANC is like his favourite soccer team, Manchester United: going through a tough time and causing him heartache, but a team he'll stay loyal to. Presumably the DA is his Arsenal.

The Arms Deal

politics / controversy

So much has been written about the 1999 Arms Deal, including a decade and a half of newspaper headlines and a number of good books – try *After The Party* by Andrew Feinstein for the insider's account, or *The Devil In The Detail* by Paul Holden and Hennie van Vuuren for the comprehensive overview – that it seems like cruelty to trees to add more. And yet it has become such an ingrained and definitive feature of the South African political landscape that it seems impossible not to include it here. So, we'll keep it short. Here is a 140-character description of the Arms Deal, for the modern, Twittering world:

ANC's original sin in power. Party tainted, JZ hounded, only Yengeni jailed (briefly). Overpaid, got the wrong stuff, submarines don't work.

That's 140 on the nose, full stops included. Would have loved to add "and half the Gripen fighter jets, which cost about R500 million each, are in long-term storage because we can't afford to fly them" – but that didn't quite fit.

"Babalas"

So you were totally amped for the jol, but then you ended up getting gesuip and a little dronk verdriet and now you've got the droogies and a moerse babalas…

In other words, you were originally excited for the party, but you ended up rather intoxicated, and even a bit tired and emotional, and now you are beset with a somewhat dry mouth and a hangover that may be the death of you.

Babalas: a marvellous Zulu-originated term – from *ibhabhalazi*, for hangover – the mellifluous sound of which does little to soothe the nausea rising in your gullet and the pack of miniature barking dogs in your head.

Bergies

Bergie used to be a Cape Town-specific word for a homeless person who lived on the mountain (the *berg*). Nowadays, bergie is known countrywide and can be applied to anyone who lives on the streets; our word for vagrant or hobo. But the best bergies are still in Cape Town. They are the bums of the city, and of the multitudes of South African poor out there who live a hand-to-mouth existence, the average bergie probably gets the biggest bum deal. He doesn't even have a shack for a home, there's no way he's on the waiting list for a government RDP house, he gets harassed by the cops for sleeping under bridges and in flower pots and by aghast suburbanites for going through their garbage, and he's not landing himself a *Big Issue* vending gig any time soon. Yet he is a free spirit – not for a bergie the trappings of modern living – and he is also possessed of some truly unique skills. He can swear in 34 of our 11 official languages, he can sleep in the baking midday sun on the side of the highway with cars going by at 100km/h, he can drink a 5-litre papsak of wine the day after sieving a half-bottle of meths through a loaf of white bread without going blind, he knows several obscure forms of karate, he almost never takes a multivitamin, he *owns* a trolley race, and he can wear his entire wardrobe in one go. He can also have a full conversation with himself, complete with introduction, narrative arc, an argument of some sort, emotional resolution and celebratory drink at the end. Some people might call it madness, but for a guy mired in virtually complete socioeconomic tragedy, at least he's got an upbeat attitude.

Biltong

Biltong. Billies. Billoes. 'Tong.

Dried meat. Sometimes spicy, sometimes not. Chewy. Best friend of the Atkins dieter. Best partnered with droëwors (dried sausage). National obsession. Can be a mystery to foreigners. (It's just dried meat, right? No, foreigners, it's biltong.) Mainstream options are beef (standard), kudu and springbok (tastier), and ostrich (recommended for vegetarians). Can, however, be any antelope that walks the earth. Equally acceptable as a breakfast offering or bedtime snack. Everyone can eat it, from teething babies to toothless geriatrics. Available everywhere – including supermarket-checkout queues, pharmacies, petrol stations, gyms, bars, the movies, the side of the road, online and at an antiques shop in Stellenbosch. Not recommended from those purveyors (except maybe the antiques shop), though they'll do in an emergency. Rather try your local butcher, dedicated biltong shop or your own garage.

In summary, biltong is delicious. If you have a differing opinion, best keep it to yourself, foreigner.

Boerewors v braai wors

Boerewors, like biltong, is a South African delicacy. No braai is complete without it. You may as well have a sandwich without the bread, or a threesome without the third person. Thing is, if you're going to have boerewors – and, as you can see, we recommend you do – you need to make sure it's actual boerewors, not braai wors or braai sausage or anything else with a suspiciously non-boerewors-sounding name. In South Africa there are government regulations stipulating what may or may not be included in sausage that is labelled boerewors. It's got to be 90 percent meat, of which no more than 30 percent can be fat. It can't be made from offal (except the casing) or mechanically recovered meat (gross), and nothing but cereal products, spices, permitted flavourants, vinegar and water may be added. Braai wors, on the other hand, could be anything. *Anything*.

Born-frees

politics / people

Technically, the born-frees are South Africans who were born after 27 April 1994; that is, born into a free and democratic country. Importantly, goes the thinking, we'll be getting our first wave of them voting in 2014, a potential elections game changer. With no memory of life under apartheid rule or the ANC as a liberation organisation (rather than ruling party), is the born-free a new voter unencumbered by the political trappings of our past? Will he or she represent a clean break from the ideologies that shaped the rest of our (now-biased) political thinking?

Possibly... But then what's the difference if you were born on 28 April 1994 versus, say, 10 April the same year? Or how about 10 April 1993, or 11 February 1990?* Surely, those four years can't offer too much opportunity for ideological indoctrination – and yet you would have been eligible to vote in 2009.

So maybe it's a sliding scale then, and you could, for the sake of this argument, run it back to include anyone who was not yet in high school when FW de Klerk started winding down the apartheid state in the late '80s. What you'd have then are South Africans under the age of 35 – and all this dovetails rather conveniently with the age group surveyed in September 2013 by consumer research company Pondering Panda… Please bear with us a little longer because there is a point coming and it is almost within touching distance.

And the point is this. Regardless of race or gender, just one in ten South Africans between the ages of 18 and 34 finds our politicians trustworthy. This is a quite instructive finding and it implies – perhaps – that the other nine out of ten young voters are going to need some real persuading come election time, and that the people in charge (see **The ANC**) are going to have to start winning their support by delivering good governance, rather than relying on decades-old loyalty and food-parcel handouts. Given that there will be around five to six million new born-frees at every election from here on, this is a phenomenon that will only have a greater and greater effect in the future.

Well, that's the theory, and if it's only half accurate then it sure is something to be hopeful about. Just don't read the **Youth unemployability** entry now…

* 11 February 1990: Mandela released. 10 April 1993: Chris Hani assassinated. Dates to know even if you weren't born then.

Braais

food / heritage

There are certain things in every culture that are sacred and should never be ridiculed. To an American, it's his national flag. To a Frenchman, it's wine and garlic. And to a South African, it's the Braai. To avoid getting a tong in the eye, it's imperative that overseas visitors stick to the following Braai rules.

- When writing the word Braai here, it takes a capital B indicating its importance in the world. Like God.
- Never demean a Braai by calling it a barbecue. It is a Braai, and only a Braai. (A barbecue is a sauce; not a very good one.)
- Even though Afrikaners invented the word*, Braais are loved by all South Africans. *All* of them. Afrikaners, rooineks, whites, blacks, young, old, men, women. Women, in particular, love the opportunity to spend time together in the kitchen making salads.
- Men at a Braai stand around the fire and discuss important matters, such as meat, sport, beer and the like. Women drink wine elsewhere. With ice. Maybe while making the salad if they want, but that's really up to them.
- Don't have the audacity to stand around a Braai and talk about how much more convenient a gas Braai is. Gas Braais aren't Braais, they're outside ovens.
- There are many different types of Braai. Don't bring cubed vegetable kebabs and a bottle of Rosé to a Man Braai. (You may bring a mielie if you haven't taken off the leaves already.)
- Unless you are the Braai Master, you may not touch the coals or the meat. Especially if it's a potjie. This is science, my friend.
- Meat is served rare to medium-rare from the Braai. Anything else is messing with the vibe. But this rule may be voided if the Braai Master has consumed more than ten double brannas en cokes** or 12 Black Label quarts, in which case the meat will likely be charred to ash on one side and alive on the other.
- The inherent awesomeness of a Braai does not necessarily mean the food will be good. See paragraph above.

- A Braai can take place anywhere. Including and especially from the boot of your car at a sporting event.
- It's never too cold / hot / humid / windy / earthquake-y / early / late / soon since your last Braai to have a Braai.
- There has been recent controversy over the fact that Heritage Day is becoming known as Braai Day in some circles. Heritage Day should not be known as Braai Day. It is plain wrong. *Every day* is Braai Day.

* Braai comes from the Afrikaans word braaivleis [*braai*: roast + *vleis*: meat]
** Brandy and coke. Can substitute with spook 'n' diesel (cane and coke) or John Deere (cane and cream soda). Or a Busta (whisky and Fanta grape) if you must.

The bush

places / paradise

B is a letter of classic Saffer favourites. We've had biltong, braais and boerewors – now one that's not a food: the bush. The bush is the wild. Kruger, Madikwe, Hluhluwe, the Kalahari. It's where old-school Africa exists. Lions and elephants and crocodiles and survival of the fittest. It's the cry of a fish eagle and the grunt of hippos. It's checking your shoes for scorpions and it's a cobra on the sofa when you get back from a game drive. It's magic.

Even if he never goes to the bush and even if he doesn't consciously know it – even if he grew up on a hippy commune in Knysna or is a Benoni beefcake who lives for the gym – a South African's soul longs for the bush. And if he moves overseas, heaven forbid, then his soul will only long for the bush even more.

Bush, as opposed to *the* bush, is something else altogether and it's great too. Especially in that hippy commune in Knysna.

[See **Lowveld sunsets**]

Cape Town

Cape Town is chilled, man. Cape Town is the Mother City. Cape Town is the mountain and the sea. Cape Town is one of the most beautiful cities in the world, a place of natural wonder and interconnected energies, where the beaches are pristine, the food is sublime and fine wine flows from the vineyards at its doorstep.

Cape Town is so completely up its own arse it's frightening.

If Cape Town were a drug it would be pure MDMA – something that leaves you utterly content and euphoric in your own little world, while people around you who are not on your exact, specific wavelength think you're a frikken self-absorbed weirdo who keeps touching his face. Then again, if you're from the wrong side of the Kaapstad tracks, your drug of choice is more likely to be tik, the city's own special brand of crystal meth, which does wonders for your complexion and will almost certainly have some influence on your future schmodelling career.

Which is all to say that, if you're not looking at it from the inside, Cape Town is a smug bubble of unfriendly, aloof, shallow, Euro-gangster wannabes who can't drive for shit and who like to think they're oh-so-special with their famous mountain and their famous island and their roads that don't have potholes and their billing system that works. And fine, their beaches are all white and quite nice, but have you ever dipped your toe into the sea at Clifton? Have you? It's like an ice cream headache for your foot. You may as well cover yourself in liquid nitrogen it's so cold. What's the point of a beach if you can't even bloody swim?

P.S. Don't be a hater, man. Cape Town is the best and you know it.

Car guards people / stereotypes

The best car guards in the business have the ability to – while high on glue, and using only indecipherable hand gestures, whistles and the phrases *Woza chief* or *Come bossy* – guide you into a space that is five cars' long and a blind person could park in it, then vanish entirely from the scene right as a group of undesirables wander into view, only to magically reappear at your car window, a bit like Keyser Söze, the moment you return, asking for money but having provided no service whatsoever. If you're looking for parking before a major sporting event, they will run next to your car for a kilometre before you find a spot that they then claim is in their jurisdiction and it costs R50 to park here, chief. Bless them.

Meanwhile, the car guards that actually provide a service are likely Central African refugees with postgraduate qualifications, who have taken charge of entire parking lots in major urban areas.

The service they provide is, of course, supplying cocaine and other narcotics, but your car should be fine parked with them.

Cars & cellphones

Cars and cellphones: the two greatest status symbols in SA. The car thing is the big one obviously. It's a car so it's going to be expensive – and your average Saffer will happily spend a quarter or more of his salary to make it as expensive as possible. The mortgage? No, he rents with mates or still lives at home. Just as long as there's a Merc C180 or a BMW 3 Series in the driveway.

Cellphones are clearly far cheaper, but they're not just portable telephones; they are themselves portable cars – because you can't drive your Merc into the club. So out comes the latest phone, as big as your face, that can control the Large Hadron Collider – and, of course, the flashier the person, the more likely he's on pay-as-you-go and had to pay R12,000 cash for the thing.

And the irony of it all: we're the worst drivers in the world and our cellphone coverage has become so bad you can barely make calls any more. Still, you have to laugh when the madam gets jealous that her maid's got the iPhone 5S and she's only got the 5.

[See **Driving**]

Carte Blanche-induced Sunday night Loser's Complex

"You can never really enjoy Sundays because at the back of your mind you know you have to go to school the next day." Such is the wisdom of *Calvin And Hobbes*. If you wanted to adapt that little aphorism as a South African adult with a job to go to on Mondays, you might say something like, "You can never really enjoy Sunday evenings if you watch *Carte Blanche* because, by the end of it, you'll be quite close to murdering yourself."

For those who haven't watched M-Net at any stage in the last 25 years, *Carte Blanche* is an award-winning "magazine and actuality" programme that runs for an hour before the Sunday-night movie premiere. It's possibly the most professionally produced, well-run local show on television. But, man, is it depressing as hell. Especially if you've had a big Saturday night out and you've been processing not only a hangover, but also feelings of bashfulness and possibly shame during the course of the day. This is because *Carte Blanche* creates content that is scientifically proven to play up to every heartstring-pulling, self-absorbed, middle-class neurosis imaginable. By the time you've sat through a segment on old-age-home nurses abusing their geriatric patients (how could they?), an interview with an expert on species extinction (how could we?) and an exposé on Malicious Mother Syndrome (how could *anyone*?), your depressive levels will be off the charts. You will be disgusted with the state of the world around you, the people you call your friends, and yourself for, among other things, ordering a large pizza with extra salami and a 2-litre Coke and inhaling it all in five minutes. You may even be in tears.

Never fear, my friend. You simply have *Carte Blanche*-induced Loser's Complex, or LCs. If it's a bad case you may be what is technically referred to as swimming in the Elsies River… Because Elsies sounds like LCs… Don't worry, anyone could miss that. You're not a loser. It's fine. You're fine. You and the other 500,000 people who watched the show.

The Constitution

The South African Constitution: possibly the best constitution in the world. Just have to keep it that way and we're all good.

(Worth reading the preamble, at least.)

Crime & corruption

The former is why many South Africans emigrated during the 1990s and early 2000s. The latter is what the people who thought about emigrating but chose to stay vex about the most these days.

While still inordinately high by world standards, crime in South Africa appears to have dropped quite significantly in recent years. In 1994 our murder rate was around 67 people per 100,000; by 2013 it was down to 31 per 100,000 – an enormous drop aided by the end of a virtual civil war in KwaZulu-Natal and the removal of our (corrupt) national police commissioner who publicly wondered what all the fuss about crime was. (Direct quote: "What's all the fuss about crime?" – Jackie Selebi.) Despite these improvements, we remain one of the most murderous countries in the world and have a long, long way to go in the general crime-fighting department.

Meanwhile, our corruption levels are relatively handy by world standards, with South Africa coming in at a solidly mediocre 43/100 on Transparency International's global Corruption Perceptions Index for 2012, and placing comfortably in the top 40 percent of 174 countries rated, below Saudi Arabia but above Italy. Yet there seems to be a growing sense that South Africa's state coffers have become an open trough for our politicians, and their friends and families, to loot at will. And it's a perception that's not helped by a president mired in corruption allegations of his own, from the decade-old Arms Deal case to recent questions about his private residence.

So what we need is to continue the (relatively) good work on the crime front and then nail the corruption problem. Maybe hold a Truth and Reconciliation Commission for the Arms Deal and then actually fire politicians who are bust with their fingers in the till (rather than briefly suspending them or moving them about or doing nothing whatsoever). Problem is it would never work. Because we're whingers. Even if we solved both these epic disasters with the most magical of magic bullets, we'd still find something to complain about.

[See **The unlawful police**]

Nkosazana Dlamini-Zuma people / politics

If, for whatever unforeseen and/or Machiavellian reason, the political gods decree that Cyril Ramaphosa should not be the next president of South Africa, in 2019, then it will most likely be Nkosazana Dlamini-Zuma (or Julius Malema). As in, the current chairwoman of the African Union and the ex-wife of a certain Jacob Zuma. So look out for her name in the news. And don't worry, she's not half bad.

(Jokes about Malema, by the way. He has more chance of winning the Egte Vrystaat Boere Woodwork Competition than being our next president.)

[See **The Home Affairs revolution, Cyril Ramaphosa** and **Helen Zille**]

Driving

Driving in South Africa is an affliction – a mental affliction with physical manifestations. The mental part is a complex combination of the African wild-frontier attitude to life in general, the schizoid frustrations and insecurities of a First World / Third World society, and the vast oceans of repressed rage that boil over the moment our hands are placed firmly on a steering wheel. The physical manifestations come, of course, in the unqualified mayhem that plays out on our roads every day, due to any number of reasons: our enduring fondness for cutting in at exits, our inability to use our indicators with any vestige of competence whatsoever, our absolute unawareness of anyone else around us, and the like. Throw in the kind of (often drunk) pedestrian who believes he has as much right to the road as a (probably speeding) delivery van, and it's carnage. Special awards to the long-distance driver who has a penchant for overtaking on blind uphills, the Joburg minibus taxi that *drives down the wrong side of the road during rush-hour traffic*, and the oblivious cellphone-yakking SUV soccer mom who is hopeless. Just hopeless.

Durban

places / city

Durbs is great. Durbs is hundreds. Or, if you prefer, it's lukker. Not lekker; *lukker*. Because Durbs is just a bit different to the rest of SA, you check. The majority population group in Durbs is Zulu but there are loads of charous – one in five Durbanites, my cuzzie, and there are actually more charous (that is, Indians) in Durbs than in any city outside India, so you know you're getting the best curry west of Mumbai. And, unlike in the other big cities, the white ous in Durbs can speak a bit of Zulu and with the whole Indian influence they have their own vocab and you can jigga with the language, you know? And they're friendly as anything in Durbs, even if by mistake you wander into downtown where, let's be honest, it's more like Dirt-bin and your chances of being mugged are a little on the high side.

Besides Zulus and Indians, Durbs is full of buggers. You might think that if Durbs were a drug it would be Durban poison, or some or other strain of dagga, and we could have a zol together and you could tune me how your idea makes sense. But you'd be wrong. Because if Durban were a drug it would be cane and Coke. Or cane and cream soda. Or possibly cane and Sparletta. Yes, cane combined with a high-sugar mixer is technically not a drug, but in Durban it is. And, man, do those buggers love a cane to go with their rugby. Because, of course, Durban is home to the Sharks. Which means Durbanites are the most insufferable rugby supporters on the planet – which is a bugger, bugger.

Still, the beaches are great and the water is warm.

"Dwaal" (as a cool Afrikaans-English word)

language / vocab

Afrikaans, as a language, has its fair share of critics. And we're not just talking Sowetan schoolchildren circa 1976. Perhaps most harshly, Afrikaans has been looked down on by speakers of its parent language, Dutch, since the 18th century or thereabouts, when it began morphing from the original High Dutch that arrived with Jan van Riebeeck. The language of the Cape came to be known, not particularly surprisingly, as Cape Dutch, but it eventually acquired far less flattering sobriquets; one of the kinder ones was Kitchen Dutch, suggesting that it was no better than the language spoken by servants and slaves who prepared the food. (No guesses where the racial superiority thing came from, then.) Even today when you try speaking a bit of Afrikaans to an enlightened Amsterdam native, he may treat you like a cretin or perhaps a small child. Still, for all its guttural unpleasantness, double negatives and simpleton grammar, Afrikaans vocabulary is jam-packed with life, attitude and what the French might call a certain I-don't-know-what. Influenced by Malay, Portuguese and any number of indigenous African languages, there are specific Afrikaans words, with no English equivalent, that magically encapsulate an idea and thus have become an integral part of (and have evolved within) South African English. One of them is dwaal.

A dwaal is a state of dopey absent-mindedness that's usually rather pleasant. So if you're in a dwaal your mind has wandered off to nowhere in particular and you're pretty much zoned out. Your eyes may be open, staring blankly into the middle distance, and you may have a faintly content smile on your face. At this point if someone calls your name (he'll have to do it several times), your likely response when he finally gets your attention will be, *Hmm?* As in:

Randy. Ra-andy. Randy! Randy!!
Hmm? You talking to me?
Yes, I'm talking to you. What the hell's up with you?
Sorry, man, I was in a bit of a dwaal.

Dwaal is a great word and dwaals themselves are pretty cool. Capetonians are in them a lot of the time.

[See **"Kak"**, **"Moer"**, **"Voetsek"** and others]

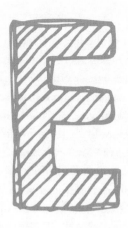

EFF

Oh Julius, you're such a kidder.

When Julius Malema launched his new political party, the Economic Freedom Fighters – with its hilariously appropriated AZAPO/NUM mash-up logo and its dunce-cap red berets – a lot of cynical observers made jokes that EFF must stand for EFF-off or get-EFFed or you-must-be-EFFing-crazy. But we all know Julius was really fondly remembering his matric exams.

"Eish"

language / vocab

Apparently derived from Tsotsitaal in the '90s, *eish* is a great example of the post-democracy evolution of South African English. Though it is only the fourth most-spoken first language in the country – behind Zulu, Xhosa and Afrikaans – English has assumed the position of the lingua franca of our media, politics and business. Which means more people are speaking it and it's open to more influence. Hence eish.

Much like its close cousin hayibo, eish is used to express a whole gamut of reactions, though generally it's the more downbeat of the two words – so it's more likely to be frustration, bewilderment, resignation and the like. And ever since those wily Klipdrift advertisers cleverly used it to sell their product – introducing, in the process, the phrase "Met eish ja" as a way to ask for ice (ys) in your drink – it can now have a bit of a contemplative or ruminative element to it as well. Basically it can represent just about any emotion you want. Up to you, really.

[See "Hayibo"]

English sports teams

sport / rivalry

When it comes to the three major South African sports codes, the teams we can't abide losing to are as follows:

Soccer: Nigeria and England
Rugby: New Zealand and England
Cricket: Australia and England

This is not to say we like losing to anyone else – we're South Africans; if we weren't competitive by nature our ancestors would've been eaten by black-backed jackals – but those are our prime antagonists, the teams that bring about the most intensely vexatious, and often public, meltdowns when we suffer at their hands. Most of them make the list because they're the best teams around and hard to beat. But the reasons for the common denominator on all three lists, England, go far deeper than that.

Essentially, when it comes to sporting confrontations, we despise the English more than any people in the world. You'd think that black and Afrikaans South Africans might drive this national sentiment, what with colonialism and the Boer wars and that, but in reality it's English-speaking South Africans who are riled the most by the Poms – and the explanation is a little complex. Certainly there's some show-up-the-motherland spite in there, but it goes deeper than that. It's really about their supporters and their press and how stridently one-eyed and reaching they all are – and how that, in turn, transforms their players into the biggest walking penises on earth.

Whether it's wildly overstating their football team's chances at the next major tournament (English press: "How can we lose?!". Reality: "You'll lose. In a penalty shootout") or claiming how incomparably brilliant their cricket team is on the first morning of a three-test series, the English media alone are enough to drive an outsider demented. That first example happens before every single World Cup and Euro, but that second one was specific to the Proteas tour of England in 2012, when several Sky Sports commentators declared that, man for man, only three, or perhaps four, Proteas would make a combined England-South Africa XI. Happily we beat them 2-0 in the series – but the aggravation levels were off the charts at the time.

The Poms aren't half ruthless either: if England win, the whole team gets knighted and feted as heroes forever; but if they lose, then those same heroes become pariahs in their own land, mercilessly dissected in national headlines. Even South Africans, not the most forgiving sports fans, can't get their heads around this.

Problem is, they do win things from time to time. And when this happens they are insufferable. Especially if it's a foreign-born player who's done the winning, as it so often is. In July 2013 there was a period of a matter of days in which the British Lions (basically the Welsh) beat the Wallabies, Andy Murray (a Scot) won Wimbledon, Chris Froome (a South African-educated Kenyan) claimed the yellow jersey in the Tour de France before going on to win the race, and Graeme McDowell (from Northern Ireland) won the French Open golf. It was unbearable.

Perhaps if we didn't all work in the UK in our twenties and have family and friends there to email us the latest Stephen Jones rugby analysis, English sports teams might be easier to handle. As it is they have a football team filled with spineless, overpaid Premier League divas who tremble at the thought of a penalty shootout; their rugby team is a collection of the finest public-school twats known to humanity; and their cricketers… Well, you don't need to say much more than "Stuart Broad", really, to define the worst sun-shines-out-of-my-own-bum attitude. The only decent ones in that team are the ex-Saffers. Except, of course, for Kevin Pietersen. Who, we can all agree, is the world's biggest douchebag.

The evolution of kwaito

Kwaito is township, and township is kwaito.

Kwaito is the music of black youth culture. It is kwaai, it is cool and it is gangster. And it is the most important and influential music movement to have emerged in South Africa in the last two decades (though the Boere electro-pop fans might argue).

Much as the Bronx is considered the home of hip-hop, so Soweto is the birthplace of kwaito, circa 1993 or 1994 or thereabouts, a time of euphoric political transition and not a little mayhem and uncertainty. Out of this brew came Mzansi's own hip-hop style, driven by heavy drumbeats and driving bass lines, layered with dreamy synthesisers and feisty hi-hat riffs, and punctured by often angsty vernacular lyrics that spoke to the previously disenfranchised and still-frustrated youth. It drew on a number of sources, such as the *mbaqanga/maskhandi* of the '50s, disco rhythms of the '80s and mid-tempo house music of the '90s, straddling all these genres to create something new, vibrant and kicking. (If you're wondering, white people did not have a clue what the hell was going on when they heard it.)

And so emerged a group of artists that spoke to the hopes and ambitions of the township's younger generation. You couldn't turn a corner in Soweto without being harassed by the sounds of Trompies, Brothers of Peace, Boom Shaka, Arthur or TKZee. But not all kwaito music had a political message. As the genre developed, it became slicker, better produced, more popular and, inevitably, more poppy – so much so that it was eventually criticised for steering clear of politics. But it still formed an integral part of *lokshin** culture and, of course, entertainment. From kwaito artists spinning their coveted *gusheshe** while drinking their Zamalek* to dancers performing the trademark *pantsula**, kwaito was an extension of the ghetto, a frenetic art form with infectious rhythms that blared from boomboxes and oversized taxi sound systems.

And then they started playing it at sports events.

Not all kwaito songs, mind you. One song in particular. One song that would become the de facto stadium anthem of South Africa, perhaps even usurping Johnny Clegg's *Impi*. One that was popular enough to cross the gaping musical colour chasm – to be warmly embraced by the average kwaito fan's lighter-hued brethren (who had finally got it) – but still managed to retain a modicum of street cred. The song in question: *Nkalakatha* by Mandoza, the chart-topping 2001 South African Music Awards Song of the Year, which has evolved, in the past decade, from township hit to massive bestseller to stadium anthem to rugby- and cricket-match cliché…

These days, Mandoza and his fellow '90s pioneers are relics by music-industry standards, and younger upstarts like Big Nuz and DJ Cleo have taken up his mantle. And now we wait in anticipation for one of them to come up with something new and astounding that will allow *Nkalakatha* to be sent to kwaito heaven. Given that ancient hits like *Get Ready For This* and *Living Next Door To Alice* still make the stadium playlists, and that the St George's Park brass band thinks *Sexy Eyes* is the business, and that the pinnacle of South African sports chants is *Olé, olé, olé*, we're not exactly holding our breath.

(As for *Heeeeeeey-ey Baby, ooh–ah, I wanna knooooow…* is that the worst song of all time? Quite possibly.)

* Vocab rundown:

lokshin *n.* apartheid-era townships were known as *lokasies* (locations) by the authorities of the day, abbreviated to lokshin and kasi by locals

gusheshe *n.* the BMW E30, or 325i as it's more popularly known; has become a cult township car for its ability to effortlessly spin its rear wheels, which allows for the performance of all sorts of life-threatening and much-admired stunts

Zamalek *n.* Carling Black Label, beer of choice in the townships; named, it is said, for the Egyptian football club Zamalek after they'd beaten Soweto giants Kaizer Chiefs – because both were so strong…

pantsula *n.* dance styled on kwaito beats; derived from *mapantsula*, meaning small-time gangster and later a fashionable young urban black person

Fast food

food / horrors

Considering that we're one of the fattest countries in the world, with perhaps 45 percent of the population being overweight or obese* (here's looking at you, Khulubuse Zuma), it really shouldn't come as much of a surprise that fast food is a colossal industry in South Africa. Though it may not have functioning streetlights, even our most backward one-horse town will have at least one fast-food restaurant to service its local inhabitants and passing commuters. Fact of the matter is we're a nation that loves our deep-fried, saturated, sugary, sodium-laden foods – as is evident in the continued nationwide success of the fast-food franchise industry and the modern notion that Spur steakhouses and Ocean Basket seafood restaurants are virtual fine-dining establishments.

A step down the food chain from those two are the real fast-food brands: Wimpy, Steers, McDonald's, King Pie, Pie City, Debonairs, Panarottis – but that's not forgetting the journeyman chains that can still dominate a Lydenburg shopping centre or National road pitstop: BJ's, Bimbo's, Mimmos, Scooters, St Elmo's, Something Fishy, Fontana, Whistle Stop… And the arrival of Burger King to our shores in 2013 only elevated fast-food fanaticism to new heights, with offers of free burgers for the first thousand customers. The result? Droves of expectant customers queuing for days on end… to try out a Whopper Burger. Talk about devotion to the cause.

Subway sandwiches are also popular, though a little too healthy for our tastes. Rather, your average Saffer fast-food sandwich-lover prefers a locally inspired creation. In Cape Town it's a Gatsby, an enormous French loaf filled with slap chips**, one or several cuts of meat (polony, viennas, rat tails, whatever), various extras (onions, beans, etc) and half a dozen oozing, heart-crystalising sauces. Gatsbys are, according to their devotees, great. In Durban it's bunny chow that gets them going. Take a loaf of white bread, cut off an enormous section, pull out the middle stuff and fill it with curry – then use the bits you've pulled out to dunk back in… And in Soweto, substitute the curry for anything grossly unhealthy, call it a kota (as in, a quarter loaf) and you've got a similar result.

But it's the Chicken Giants that truly astound. From the small-fry Hungry Lion, with only a hundred-plus outlets across the country, to the seriously successful Chicken Licken, the global powerhouse that is KFC, and our very own international fast-food sensation, Nando's, with its flame-grilled peri-peri goodness and always-perceptive ads, chicken is king of the fast-food game. Bottom line: South Africans consume more than one billion chickens each year… How ballistic is that?

If you're still not sure how much South Africans love fast food, just ask supersized Northern Cape premier Sylvia Lucas how much fast food she bought on her governmental credit card during her first ten weeks on the job. She probably won't tell you, but we will: R53,159. In ten weeks. It wasn't all for her, apparently (hopefully!), but when you see pictures of her you might find that hard to believe. There are some that show her with four chins. Honestly. The one starts at her collarbone.

[See **I lo-o-o-ve su-u-u-gaaaaar**]

---

* The statistics appear to vary quite substantially, depending on the source and criteria. Figures released by the SA Medical Research Council in 2013 show that 29 percent of men and 56 percent of women are overweight. An astounding three in ten women between the ages of 30 and 60 are obese. Not overweight, obese.

** **slap chips** *n.* pale, soft, insipid-looking French fries, usually drowned in vinegar; another SA fast-food speciality

Finding coconuts

people / stereotypes

Of the many Waspish worries that concern your average English-speaking South African – and there really are so many things to worry about; watch *Carte Blanche* to be sure – one of them is his or her lack of black friends. And we don't just mean black friends, we mean *black* black friends. Because finding a black friend who hasn't been ruined by model-C education and American TV is no mean feat. See, our black buddies tend to be even whiter than us, with their beautiful accents, their love of risotto and vintage Ralph Lauren clothing, and their excess Twitter usage. (The Black Label ads don't show a bunch of guys huddled around their phones and slapping themselves on the back for being retweeted, do they?) So how does one find a guy in a woollen hat worn at a jaunty angle, and chewing on a matchstick? Someone who rolls his Rs when he says the word gravy and puts an "i" in front of everything, not just Apple products; a guy who hates dogs and doesn't leave the bones behind when eating KFC. Apparently we have a lot of them living here in Mzansi. Or maybe coconuts really are racial stereotyping at its worst? Uh-oh.

The fracking Karoo politics / controversy

Besides the actual Israel/Palestine debate, the Karoo-fracking debate is the Israel/Palestine debate of contemporary South Africa. On one side you have what appears to be a bunch of self-serving, self-delusional sociopaths and on the other side you have the Big Oil companies. Of course, they too are self-serving sociopaths (as corporations, almost by definition, tend to be), which means that any engagement between campaigners against and proponents of fracking – whether on air, online or around the braai – has a strong chance of ending in a "You're wrong, asshole!" bunfight. Check out any of Ivo Vegter's pot-stirring articles on the topic on the *Daily Maverick* for a taste. The best comments are the ones that start along the lines of "I don't know all the details, but…"

So, is the Karoo about to be plundered and polluted in the name of capitalist exploitation or are Shell and Co about to kickstart a much-needed economic boom for the country while solving our medium-term energy problems and maintaining ethical extraction practices in the process? I don't know all the details, but I have to say I'm glad the hippies at the Treasure Karoo Action Group have put up a fight. Because there's now at least a chance that their efforts will produce a measure of governmental oversight when the fracking begins. Not betting on it, though.

Fynbos

Table Mountain is, quite obviously, something. Even begrudging Vaalies can concede that much. And the sea – that's definitely nice to look at, they agree. But what, they ask, is the big deal about fynbos? Proteas are unique, sure. They are interesting. But gloriously spectacular? Perhaps if you're a protea expert. And the rest of it is just shrubs! It doesn't even provide shade!

It can be a bit of a bugbear for Joburgers that no-one ever acknowledges the beautiful aspects of their city. All outsiders ever notice are the mine dumps, billboards and squatter camps. Yet within the steel and slate and concrete lies the largest man-made forest in the world, and a sunset looking from the Polo Lounge at the Westcliff down towards the zoo is special. When the jacarandas are in bloom it's something to behold. And don't forget that money is very pretty to look at too. So when Joburgers are told that fynbos is amazing they don't buy it.

Truth is, fynbos is an acquired taste.

Never mind all those botanists going on about how the Cape floral kingdom is one of only six floral kingdoms in the world, and it has 9,000 identified species, 70 percent of which are endemic, and the Cape Peninsula alone is home to more species of plant than the entire United Kingdom… Yes, they're an excitable bunch and you still think it's shrubs.

Just go spend some time on it. It's like coffee the first time you tried it. Or anchovies. Or golf. Or single-malt whisky. They all needed a bit of perseverance.

Start in spring in front of a bright pink bank of vygies and check out the watsonia oasis on the way up Lion's Head. By the time you find a Cape disa at the top of Skeleton Gorge you'll be good.

Gaartjies

As we know, Cape Town is special (see **Cape Town**). If you need to catch a minibus taxi anywhere else in the country you hail one on the side of the road and hand your money over to the driver, usually via other passengers. Simple. But in Cape Town this setup doesn't fly, so the driver has a second-in-command, a right-hand man known as a gaartjie. Directly translated, he is the little guard, and he handles all the admin. So you pay the gaartjie, not the driver. Hell, in Cape Town you don't even look at the driver.

Why Cape Town drivers need a gaartjie is something of a mystery. Maybe it's because Kaapies don't work hard enough to do two things at once. Maybe it's because there are so many gangsters in the place that you really do need the protection. Or maybe it's because Cape locals are so deurmekaar* they need to be reminded that they need a trip somewhere – which is why your average gaartjie spends most of his life hanging out the window shouting

44 ■ Ja Well No Fine

"Mowwwwbray-Kaaaap!" or "Wiiiiiiiiine-berg!" and whistling at people in the street.

But is he, you might wonder, not taking up the space that a paying passenger might occupy? No problem; when the minibus gets full he leans so far out the window he doesn't even take up a seat.

* **deurmekaar** *adj.* confused, befuddled, not thinking straight, messed up in the head [from Afrikaans, literally "through each other"]

Game rangers

people / stereotypes

We all love a game ranger. Out in the bush, your game ranger is a god. He's the guy with the gun who'll protect you from a charging buffalo, show you the difference between serval and leopard spoor, sift knowingly through rhino dung with his fingers and explain the legend of Orion to you under a beautiful, star-spangled sky. He wears cool earthy bush clothes and sporty sunglasses, handles a Landy like a king, tells riveting stories of black mambas in the rafters, and makes all the female guests swoon (a condition known as khaki fever).

Back in the city, however, your ranger is a kudu in the headlights. He can barely operate a cellphone, he doesn't know what WiFi is and his dress sense is appalling – because it's exactly the same as it is in the bush. And though he may be able to navigate by the sun in the Kalahari desert, he can't find his way from Melville to Rosebank. He is a lost soul who can't handle the stresses of the modern world – which goes to show that, if there's any animal that belongs in the wild, it's a game ranger.

"Give that man a Bell's"

 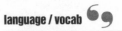

Once upon a time a lovely catchphrase to end a great little TV commercial (shot in Greyton, not Scotland, if anyone's wondering). Now an annoyingly overused figurative back-slap, associated with unfunny Facebook jokes and often-racist News24 posters giving each other emotional support.

"Gogga"

language / vocab

The English call it a mite. The Americans call it a critter. We call it a gogga, or sometimes a goggo.

A gogga is all in the pronunciation. It's not a gogga with soft Gs that rhymes with jogger – that's probably a gathering of Jewish grandmothers or something. No, it's a gogga with guttural Gs that come gurgling out the back of your throat, and it rhymes with no other word you know. This is because it has its etymological roots in the Khoikhoi word for insect, *xo-xon*.

In summary, a gogga is a cute and endearing way of describing a creepy-crawly. Bearing in mind, of course, that in South Africa a creepy-crawly is spelt Kreepy Krauly and it's the thing that cleans your pool. It's a South African invention, the Kreepy Krauly, and, come to think of it, should probably be called the gogga.

The great emigration debate

The great South African emigration debate is a classic that has been ongoing since the '70s, at least. Of course, the poor can't emigrate and the rich don't have to – they holiday in London and New York and the south of France for nine months of the year and come "home" for summer – so it is essentially a middle-class dilemma. And if you've been on either side of it, you'll know how heated it gets and how easy it is to work an expat into an internet-frothing mess by mentioning the average winter temperatures in Toronto or the suicide rate in Limerick. Similarly, South Africans who have chosen to stay – or have "chosen" to stay because they can't really leave – tend to get all heated around the collar area when they're repeatedly alerted to the latest governmental scandal, the rising cost of living, the declining rand, etc etc. There are many books about the topic – some excellent and angsty, others just angsty – but here's the précised version of the debate for those who couldn't be bothered.

The positives of living in South Africa come in the form of the four Ss: Sun, Scenery, Space and Staff.

The negatives of living in South Africa are described by the three Cs: Crime, Corruption and Crap.

Notice that there are four in the positive column and three in the negative. Case closed!

"Having a cadenza"

The literal meaning of cadenza is a virtuoso solo musical passage, but somewhere along the line, apparently in the 1940s, we adapted the phrase "having a cadenza" as a wonderful little South Africanism, and today it is a perfect descriptor for kugels and interior designers going into a flat panic.

So when Sheryl has been running around all day – from Pilates class to the Nine West shoe sale to coffee with Shannon to taking little Jaydon to extra lessons – and she barely managed to make it to Gorgeous Nailz in Sandton City in time, where she got a full set of acrylics done, and then literally as she walks in the door at home she catches her finger in the keys and breaks one of her brand-new nails – that results in a cadenza.

And when Marc-Justin has been on the phone to clients all day and sending emails and signing off invoices, and then the window cleaner opens the window so he can clean the outside, which lets in a gust of wind that blows some papers on the floor and Marc-Justin stands up, stomps his foot and declares to the room, "How am I supposed to work in these conditions?!" before grabbing his man bag and storming out – he, too, is having a cadenza.

When you're having a cadenza you're in a state of agitation and it's the end of the world. Someone or something has literally done his or its best, on purpose, to ruin your life – and you just can't cope. You - just - can't - cope.

In retrospect it's possible it wasn't such a big thing. When you think about it a bit. You wouldn't say you overreacted or anything, but you know, ja, maybe you overreacted a bit.

"Hayibo!" language / vocab

hayibo *exclam*. expression of shock, excitement, amazement, surprise, disgust, irritation and/or disbelief

Hayibo – pronounced *high-boh* – is so versatile. As is quite evident on hearing it, the word has black-language origins (in this case, Xhosa), but it rolls off the tongue with such ease and ambiguity that it has been appropriated by white South Africans everywhere, especially those who like to appear culturally accepting but don't know more Xhosa words than the lyrics to *I Am A Teapot*. (And those who are tired of using wow or yoh.)

WHITE GUY: "Hayibo! This downtown Joburg club is so dope, don't you think, Sipho?"

BLACK GUY: "Hayibo! You are a strange white man."

At its most basic level, it means No!, Go away! or You're crazy! – but it can effectively be used to express any short emotional interjection that ends with an exclamation mark. Given the state of modern punctuation, that's pretty much anything, then.

Hayibo is mainstream enough to be considered acceptable for use in English-language newspaper headlines – admittedly usually the *Sowetan* or *Daily Voice* – and most tellingly was the name given to South Africa's first satirical-news website. Started in 2008, Hayibo.com was inspired by Monty Python and *The Goon Show*, quickly became "the second-best source of made-up news after the SABC" and was regularly compared to *The Onion* and Jon Stewart's *The Daily Show*. It lambasted politicians for being politicians and it confused readers who didn't understand that reports of Liewe Heksie moving to Perth were made up. What it didn't do was make money. Could be it over-intellectualised things. Could be South Africans just can't take the piss out of themselves. Whatever the reason, it eventually went under in late 2012. Hayibo!

Or should that be eish?

[See "**Eish**"]

Highveld storms v Cape storms (v KZN tornados)
weather / patterns

Highveld thunderstorms and Cape winter cold fronts are local weather legends, the two most recognised storm types in the country. The former are short and dramatic, puncturing Gauteng summers like clockwork; the latter are lengthy and incessant, and they *are* winters in the Cape. Both are flippen fantastic.

Nothing relieves the heat of the day and cleanses the charged city atmosphere like a Highveld thundershower. In minutes the white cumulonimbus clouds over Joburg turn black, heralding at first a scatter of bullet-sized raindrops – before the entire sky comes bucketing down a few seconds later. If you're lucky you'll get thunderclaps that set off car alarms and a lightning show to put Jean Michel Jarre to shame. And if you're *really* lucky it'll be November and you'll be in a jacaranda-lined avenue with a camera-flash electric storm rippling above the treetops, bringing them to life. Afterwards, the air will be perfectly still and purple jacaranda flowers will litter the road; a cathartic sense of wellbeing will fill your soul and you'll think, Nooit, I could smash a beer at the Baron right now…

As for a beating Cape storm – well, it wasn't called the Cape of Storms for nothing. Meteorologically speaking, these are mid-latitude cyclones, and the clue to their ferocity is in the second word there: cyclone. At their best, they're biblical, with drumming, dream-destroying rain for days on end and 100km/h winds that knock over oak trees and blow ships onto the beach, and they are profound in their message. Stay the fuck inside. Watch movies. Get takeout. Hibernate. Then re-emerge in summer, a free and happy Capetonian released into the sunlight…

Meanwhile, certain parts of KwaZulu-Natal and the eastern Eastern Cape are prone to tornadoes. These storms kill people, destroy houses and have no redeeming features whatsoever.

[See **Weather misconceptions**]

Hipsters

people / stereotypes

You've seen them. Hipsters. Walking bandy-legged down the street in their liquorice-like stove-pipe pants and pixie-toed Chelsea boots like a 1950s Mickey Mouse. Thick-rimmed reading glasses, asymmetrical comb-over hairstyles, facial hair as curated as their obscure playlists. They only eat organic, grass-fed animals whose provenance they can talk about and they only drink craft beer, small-batch bourbon and Fairtrade coffee. They only wear what is found or massaged off the finest sleeping hobos, and they have maximum 5 percent body fat. They are the cool-seeking insouciant culture slugs of today's world and they are so ironically postmodern that they don't even realise how ironic they are. Which is ironic. But you don't get them, so whatever, man. They're too cool for you. They're too cool for themselves. They're so cool, in fact, that they're over it. They're over *everything*.

Hipsters are not us; except we are them. Because every single element of individual style and taste seems to have been sucked in and christened hipster – in South Africa, at least. So a tattoo of a protea is hipster. Wearing a scarf is hipster. Taking up roller skating is hipster. Wear a cardigan, get a haircut, roll a cigarette, drink a locally brewed beer, order a coffee or ride a bike without wearing spandex and someone is going to call you a hipster. Oh, you're different because you're into taxidermy? Hipster. You don't listen to obscure new music, only old classic Motown stuff? Hipster. Not wearing socks? Hipster.

Okay, that last one is totally fucking hipster, but you get what we're saying. In general the hipster label has become a lazy new term for "trying to be cool" through the way you dress, listen, eat and drink. Hey, aren't we talking about people in Cape Town then? Bloody hipsters.

The Home Affairs revolution

Home Affairs used to be like a Kafka novel. If you needed your ID or passport reissued, you'd book a day off work, get there at 4am to join the queue and hopefully leave by sundown with a tattered piece of paper in your hand signifying that you had applied for the document in question and should repeat the process in six months' time so as to enquire about its status. During the day, anything may have happened. You may have been sent on a treasure hunt. You may have taught a government official how to read. You may have been temporarily jailed for not producing your great-grandmother's birth certificate at the required moment. You may even have been sucked into a wormhole in the fingerprint queue as time came to a shuddering standstill. (That's more Arthur C Clarke than Kafka, though.)

Now it's a breeze. In and out in half an hour, the promised SMS is actually sent, and you have a brand-spanking-new passport within the fortnight. There's even a real chance someone may have smiled at you at some point in the process.

They say this is the work of Nkosazana Dlamini-Zuma, who was put in charge of the Department of Home Affairs in 2009. I say it's a miracle. Moreover, it's a similar story when it comes to renewing your driver's licence; a lunch break might be long enough to get the job done.

But if you really like your Kafka and you miss the old days then there is a way to relive the past, apparently. Be a foreigner and apply for some kind of working or extended visa. That, we're reliably informed, is still an absolute shit-show.

[See **Nkosazana Dlamini-Zuma**]

"Howzit"

The all-round all-South African greeting. Call it lazy or call it ingenious, but we've managed to abbreviate even the shortest of health enquiries – from "How is it going with you?" to "How's it going?" and finally, realising there was far too much surplus word wastage going on there, settling on a good old "Howzit?" – with the understanding that "Howzit" is not even a question necessarily, just a hello.

"I lo-o-o-ve su-u-u-gaaar"

Our curious and strained multicultural landscape is so complex, layered and all-encompassing that it sometimes seems an exercise in futility trying to work out how we're all going to unite in magic harmony to make the country a better place. What, for example, does Jan-Piet van Tonder, an Afrikaans mielie farmer outside Petrusburg in the Free State, have in common with Wellbeing Bonani, a Xhosa policeman working the night shift in Wynberg?

Easy. Sugar.

If you ever pop in to Jan-Piet's farm one day to see what his wife's cooked up for Sunday roast you'll discover an enormous array of vegetables (to go with half a ton of meat) that comes straight from Candyland: sugared sweet potatoes, honeyed butternut, caramel-soaked pumpkin fritters, cinnamon-glazed baby marrows, syrup-smeared beans, Oros-marinated carrots... Then comes dessert which, no matter what, will be overflowing with sugary, syrupy, supersweet goodness, and if there are koeksisters then you're eating a heart attack on a plate: braided dough that is deep fried and then soaked in cold syrup. Deep-fried sugar, in short. If you've still got room for cheese – you won't, but Jan-Piet's wife will be upset if you don't have any – then you can enjoy some raisin-cheddar on sugared biscuits with sweet chutney to finish off.

Meanwhile, back in Wynberg you'll meet Wellbeing early one morning when he comes to your house after a burglary. Then, when you offer him coffee, he'll say yes please, with a big smile, and ask for four teaspoons of sugar. Or five. Heaped. You will need to leave space when you pour in the water otherwise the coffee will spill when you add the sugar. Wellbeing will then tell you that, yes, he loves sugar and he pours it over everything he eats. His answer might remind you of the classic '80s ad for sugar with the jingle, "Nature gives us energy. I lo-o-ove su-u-u-gaaar!"

Indeed, we do. South Africans consume 1.5 million tons of sugar every year – more than one kilo per person per fortnight. Quite an achievement when you think about it. And when you think about Jan-Piet and Wellbeing, you have to laugh – at them, at us and at yourself. It's especially funny if you do it while drinking a can of Coke – which contains nearly ten teaspoons of sugar…

[See **Fast food**]

Indians (as a vision of successful cultural integration)

people / theory

Indian South Africans are an interesting bunch. And no, not just because they like to swim in their jeans or do wonderfully creative things to their cars. They're interesting because of their back story, which is perhaps a guiding metaphor for our little democracy.

Indentured Indians were first shipped to the Colony of Natal in the mid-19th century to work on the sugar cane plantations and later on the railways and in coal mines. They were followed by "passenger Indians" – traders and professionals who paid their own wages – and over the next half century many tens of thousands of both types would arrive. Hindus, Muslims and Christians, speaking Hindi, Gujarati, Tamil, Bhojpuri, Telugu and Urdu, they came from all over India and from a variety of different castes. Many of them would have had absolutely nothing in common and couldn't even communicate with one another.

As linguistics professor Rajend Mesthrie describes it, the result, after several decades of immigration, was a "stalemate" between the Tamil speakers from southern India and the Hindi speakers from the north. But over time, as the younger generations bonded and English became the common language, the divides broke down. Fast-forward past various major historical periods, such as the 20 years Gandhi spent here and the small matter of apartheid, and what was once an array of disparate cultures is now one, more or less. Yes, it probably took a good hundred years to get the ball rolling properly – and, of course, there are still differences in religions, traditions, slang, car-stylings and the rest between Indians around the country – but they are happy to identify as one connected grouping. Put another way, South African Indians have now become Indian South Africans. They have a multitude of idiosyncrasies and shibboleths, as does any group anywhere in the world, but they are, as journalist Nikita Ramkissoon puts it, "as South African as wors".

Perhaps there's a lesson in here for the rest of us. Hopefully it's not the fact that it took a century to achieve…

isiLanguage confusion

There are three tricky questions relating to our many official languages.

First of all, as mentioned a couple of times already, there are 11 of them, so what are they all? Go on, give it a bash…

Given up? Here they are in order of their prevalence as a home language around the country: Zulu, Xhosa, Afrikaans, English, Northern Sotho, Tswana, Sotho, Tsonga, Swazi, Venda, Ndebele.

Second, how do you actually say or write the nine Bantu languages? Is it Zulu or isiZulu? Sotho or Sesotho? Northern Sotho, Sesotho sa Leboa or Sepedi? Swazi, Swati, siSwati or Siswati? Should we be talking about isiXhosa, Setswana, Xitsonga, Tshivenda and isiNdebele?

One way of looking at it would be to say you don't call French *le français* because that's what a French speaker says, so why should Xhosa be *isiXhosa* because that's what a Xhosa speaker says? Then again, the other way of looking at it has the Constitution referring to it as isiXhosa, and in South Africa the Constitution is king, whether or not it's being a little bit PC about things. Frankly, if you can remember all 11 languages in some or other guise you've done quite well, and any good South African English dictionary will hedge its bets by including both options. So take your pick.

Even more confusing than this, though, is the final question. Why is it that we opted for 11 official languages and then inscribed our motto on the official South African coat of arms in another one altogether? (From the Khoisan language of the /Xam people, *!ke e: /xarra //ke* translates to "Diverse people unite".)

Or maybe it's not that confusing. Maybe it was a sneaky way to avoid picking one official language and pissing off the other ten.

"Ja well no fine"

 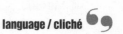

Ja well no fine, erm… "Ja well no fine" is essentially a thought prefix for Afrikaans and Afrikaans-influenced South Africans who don't know what to say. Directly translated it means "yes well no fine", but it is the semantic equivalent of "um", "er", *coughs* or …thinking… Or, in American speak, "like".

Minor variations such as "Ja no well fine" and "No well fine" are common, as is the abbreviated "Ja no", and any of these forms is likely to be heard whenever a first-language Afrikaans speaker isn't sure about how to respond to a question posed in English. This may be indicative of the fact that the speaker is perhaps slightly slow, or it's possible he's just had a long day. Technically, the answer to any question in the world posed to a South African can begin this way.

As in:

"Ja well no fine, ja." (Yes.)

"Ja well no fine, no." (No.)

"Ja no well fine, I'm fine and well, thank you." (I'm fine.)

"Ja no, Stephen. Look, that's a good question, and I could answer it in a number of ways…" (Politician's prevarication when put under pressure.)

"Jawelnofine, I fink I are seeing what you say but, er, ja… what was da question again?" (Car mechanic getting confused.)

JA WELL NO FINE. (*Cape Times* newspaper banner, September 2013 – about a busker who's fine was scrapped.)

So who's to blame for this conversational stutter? Ja well no fine, that's a difficult one to say… But not really. It's Afrikaners, plain and simple. Bless them. Because it's a beautiful thing, "Ja well no fine" – it's like Mrs Ball's or Hashim Amla; something to treasure.

Jews (as a people punching above their weight)

people / theory

Here's a random/interesting question for your next dinner-table lull in conversation: out of the world population of more than 7 billion people, how many are Jews? There are 2-billion-plus Christians, 1.5 billion Muslims, a billion Hindus, a billion or so atheists and agnostics – so how many Jews?

At this stage of proceedings – and assuming your guests are cool with the general direction the conversation is going and not neo-Nazis or affiliated to al-Qaeda in any way – you could throw in some red herrings. One in five Nobel laureates is Jewish, you could say. Steven Spielberg, you could say, and Natalie Portman, and Hollywood in general… Eventually, when they start calling you a schmuck and throwing breadsticks at you, you can tell them.

The answer is 14 million.

Only 14 million! That's less than 0.2 percent of the world population. There are twice as many Sikhs in the world as Jews. There are more Shintoists and Juche adherents than Jews. There are even more Spiritists than Jews.

What the hell, you ask, are Spiritists*?

Exactly.

Thing is, even though there are only 14 million Jews in the entire world, it sometimes feels like they're *all* shopping for shoes at Hyde Park Corner. Or perhaps half are shopping for shoes at Hyde Park Corner and the other half are in Green Point buying chicken schmaltz and bagels at Giovanni's Deliworld. Point being that the Jewish presence in South Africa is a readily felt and hugely influential one – certainly far out of proportion to their numbers.

Though a handful of their ancestors arrived with Van Riebeeck in 1652 (somewhat incognito, you'd imagine), South African Jews could only really start getting involved here from the 19th century when religious equality was introduced (kind of). They became ship-owners and ostrich farmers and diamond magnates and Randlords. Barney Barnato and Alfred Beit were major players in the Kimberley diamond rush and enhanced their fortunes on the Witwatersrand; Ernest Oppenheimer eventually controlled De Beers and started Anglo American; Johannesburg became known as "a colony of Lithuania", or even "Jewburg"; Oudtshoorn was "Little Jerusalem".

More recently, Joe Slovo, Ruth First, Helen Suzman, Albie Sachs and others played celebrated anti-apartheid roles, while

Israel itself formed a cosy little arms-dealing relationship with the Nationalist government (so yeah, no brownie points for that one). Phillip Tobias was one of the world's greatest palaeoanthropologists in the second half of the 20th century. The Rosenkowitz kids of Cape Town became the first sextuplets to survive infancy, in 1974. Jody Scheckter was Formula One World Champion in 1979. Nadine Gordimer won the Nobel Prize for Literature in 1991. Joel Stransky kicked the greatest drop goal of all time at Ellis Park in 1995…

And Pieter-Dirk Uys discovered he had Jewish heritage and promptly invented his own kugel creation, "a committed (when it suited her) liberal" during the bad old days and a post-democracy "Comrade Madam" who likes wearing Mandela-flag shirts and has interior décor tastes that lean towards "Jewish rococo". Her name is none other than Nowell Fine, and for that alone she and her fellow princesses deserve mention in these pages.

These days Jewish-influenced businesses seem to power half our economy, whether it's multinationals (Bidvest), financial services (Investec, Liberty), the legal fraternity (ENS), insurance (Discovery), steel (Macsteel), packaged goods (Tiger Brands), supermarkets (Pick n Pay, Woolworths), hospitality (Sun International), industrial and residential real estate (pretty much all of them), as well as telecoms, furniture, pharmaceuticals, retail and more. As captains of industry, they're everywhere… And, as we know, their wives and their friends are in Hyde Park Corner buying shoes – most likely while wearing leopard-print tights, a solid inch of makeup and enough gold jewellery to shame a rapper, doll.

The world's 14 million Jews do not, of course, all live in South Africa – we've got about 70,000 of them and, paralleling global statistics, they make up less than 0.2 percent of our population. As small as it is, it's the twelfth largest J-Crew population by country, but sadly – unless you're Mahmoud Ahmadinejad, or someone who dislikes lots of high-quality nail boutiques – we've had to bid farewell to a good 50,000 or more of our Jewish brothers and sisters in the last couple of decades. Many of them have hopped on the emigration boat, which is why, if you're ever in Sydney and you decide to get some sun on an eastern suburbs beach, don't be surprised when you hear, in a beautiful Sandton accent, "Hey Joshy! Josh-eee! Come here, Joshy! Put your sunscreen on, angel!"

P.S. To the worryingly large number of anti-Semitic South Africans out there who write regular letters to the papers and believe Jews control world banking, run America and conspired to arrange 9/11, this little entry is not meant to imply they're doing something similar here. It's just a big-up, really.

[See **The great emigration debate**]

* Spiritism is similar to the idea of spiritualism but an actual doctrine/religion in itself. Shinto was the state religion of Japan; Juche is the nutcase theory of North Korea that the Kims invented.

Johannesburg

places / city

Joburg is money. Joburg is business. Joburg is *the* business. Joburg is get the fuck out of my way, I'm coming through and I'll clamber over your miserable lifeless body to do it… Because Joburg is Egoli, china. It's the financial powerhouse of Africa, the greatest, most pumping city on the continent, with its biggest airport, biggest stock exchange, biggest business and biggest bigbig. It's the big time!

But Joburg is also Jozi, hey: energetic and fast and can-do and upbeat and so social you can bump into some guy in the street and he'll invite you to a braai the next day, and if you don't go he'll call you up and actually come around to pick you up from your house. Because he digs your vibe, and you're cool, bru, and you better believe it.

If Joburg were a drug it would be cocaine. Or steroids. Roids for gym, then coke for partying. And for halftime during the rugby. And a little bit for work. And also some for gym actually, come to think of it. Only a bit because, you know, you've been working on those guns and you need to take it up a notch. Feel it, feel it! Levels! Shweet, china.

But unfortunately not all of Joburg is awesome and exciting and powerful. Joburg is also dirty and dry and desiccating – especially when winter kicks in and it turns brown for half the year, and then you might just look up from your smartphone for a second to get your bearings and see that, hmm, parts of it are not very pretty (ugly as sin) and some of the architecture is a bit nouveau and OTT (sensationally bad) and the supersized billboards are really enormous and in your face, and then it dawns on you that maybe the place is a teeny bit materialistic... But then you head off to Hartebeespoort Dam for some jet-skiing for the weekend or you check out some game in Kruger and then, shweet, you're revitalised and reenergised and good to go.

Joburg. Fuck yeah.

Johannesburg,
as a world-class African city

Joburg is a "world-class African city", proclaims the City of Johannesburg. Unfortunately the Advertising Standards Authority disagrees. In July 2013 it ruled that an advert that claimed the city to be commercially stable and environmentally friendly was basically a load of bollocks. A complainant pointed out that Johannesburg had received three consecutive qualified audits, had a bankrupt waste-management service and notorious billing crisis, and was losing an estimated R24 billion a year in wasted electricity and water. As a result, the ASA found the commercial to be "misleading" and banned it.

Don't worry, though. Joburg still rocks. (See previous entry.)

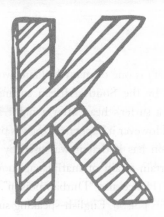

"Kak"

One of the more colourful adjectives around, and one that many South Africans can't live without. Translated from Afrikaans, kak is quite literally excrement, faeces. But rude excrement; more like crap or shit, really. In English it's not as naughty as all that and it tends to lean towards the politer side of poo, or even rubbish. But it's come to mean so much more. While chiefly considered an informal term of scorn or contempt, it seems to have become popular more as a superlative than a noun or adjective. So while someone can take a kak or be talking kak or full of kak, and something may be simply kak or a complete load of kak, and you can be having a kak time at a kak party listening to kak music to which a friend might commiserate with, "Kak one", things these days can also be kak funny, kak sad, kak long, kak cold or kak boring. It's versatile. You get the picture.

"Kiff"

Kiff (or kif or kief) is one of many brilliant words, possibly the kiffest, spawned by the South African surfing subculture. Its origins are, like a surfer's head after a night kapping zol, not altogether clear. However it happened, zol was probably involved.

One explanation has it that it was used by surfers in Natal to describe a certain strain of marijuana, known in Afrikaans as *gif* or poison. (Hence also "Durban poison".) In a hat-tip to the potency of this poison, English-speaking surfers on the east coast then started using it to describe anything that was mind-blowingly awesome, whether it was the chicks on the beach or chilling in the green room. Another possibility is that kiff is derived from the Arabic word *kayf* for pleasure or wellbeing, and that it was actually another term for marijuana or the euphoric condition that comes from smoking the drug.

Whatever the background, kiff means cool, wicked, awesome, fantastic, and a couple of decades ago it was the second word out of every kid's mouth, whether surfer or not. Though its mainstream heyday has now passed, it has enjoyed some post-ironic revival in recent years and, of course, remains a surfer standard.

[See **Who's your bru, bro?**]

KZN power

If Nelson Mandela had had his way back in the early '90s, Cyril Ramaphosa, not Thabo Mbeki, would have been his second-in-command. One of the reasons for this (among others) was Mandela's concern that too much political power would appear to rest with the Xhosa ethnic group within the ANC should Mbeki succeed him. The party's famous big three – Mandela, OR Tambo and Walter Sisulu – were all Xhosas, and so was Mbeki (and Chris Hani). Many senior ANC members at the time were, too. Ramaphosa, however, was Venda. In South Africa these things matter more than we sometimes realise. Mandela realised. But he was outmanoeuvred by Mbeki and others, and so the rise of the so-called Xhosa Nostra appeared complete when Mbeki became president in 1999.

Jacob Zuma is no Mandela. Matters of appeasing the many ethnicities within government and across the land – nation-building, some call it – would not appear to keep him up at night. Though president today, and thus the most powerful man in the country, Zuma remains (amazingly, when you think about it) within touching distance of total political downfall, not to mention a possible prison sentence, should his never-ending legal proceedings take a turn for the worse. Arms Deal corruption allegations, the mystery spy tapes, Schabir Shaik's health, what the National Prosecuting Authority is going to do next... these are, one imagines, the things that keep our president up at night. And, so the argument goes, he has done what he's genuinely good at – arranging political structures and the people around him – to ensure he avoids his day in court. This means appointing people he trusts to positions of power.

With that in mind, here is a list of *very* powerful people who walk the corridors of government and/or the ANC (in a generally descending order, as of October 2013):

- President Jacob Zuma: in charge
- ANC Secretary General Gwede Mantashe: in charge of the ANC

- Minister of Finance Pravin Gordhan: in charge of the money
- Minister of Justice Jeff Radebe: long-time power player, influences the courts
- Minister of State Security Siyabonga Cwele: in charge of spies
- Minister of Police Nathi Mthethwa: in charge of police
- Minister of Public Enterprises Malusi Gigaba: up-and-comer; potential future president
- ANC Treasurer-General Zweli Mkhize: in charge of the ANC's money
- Minister of Social Development Bathabile Dlamini: in charge of the biggest budget in cabinet by around R50 billion
- Spokesman in the Presidency Mac Maharaj: gateway to the boss.

Here is another list of genuinely powerful people who were not on the first list:
- ANC Deputy President Cyril Ramaphosa: potentially in charge one day
- ANC Chairwoman Baleka Mbete: runs ANC meetings
- ANC Deputy Secretary General Jessie Duarte: Mantashe's number two.

There are probably a handful of cabinet ministers whose noses would be put out by their exclusion here, but if we merged the lists, Ramaphosa would probably slot in below Mthethwa, and certainly no-one else merits a spot higher than that.

So, to the differentiators. People on the first list: all from KwaZulu-Natal. People on the second list: from elsewhere.

Throw in Mxolisi Nxasana, appointed in August 2013 to head the NPA – crucial when it comes to charging politicians with corruption – and that's yet another KwaZulu-Natal native in the mix. Slowly, a pattern is beginning to emerge…

Political observers sometimes talk about the modern Zulufication of the ANC, but it doesn't quite have the ring of the Xhosa Nostra and it also doesn't account for the high-powered Indians such as Gordhan and Maharaj who are close to Zuma. So what we're seeing here is the rise of KZN Power, the steady coalescing of national power within a single province. And its explanation is simple: Zuma is erecting sturdy defences around himself, whether they're trusted comrades who were underground with him in Operation Vula in the '80s or simply friendly faces from back home.

It's all quite ironic, this. In 1910 when the Union of South Africa was founded it was a time of great reconciliation between the races – between the English and the Afrikaner races, that is. In this spirit of magnanimity the power was shared among the provinces: Pretoria became the administrative capital, Cape Town the legislative capital and Bloemfontein the judicial capital. Only Natal got nothing. And now, they would appear to have almost everything.

So, is the KZN power trend a concern in terms of the day-to-day governance of the country? Not really, considering you've got some of our best-performing ministers mentioned above (though there are a couple of shockers). Is this the first step on the road to Rwandan-style ethnic genocide led by Zulu nationalists? Nope, not that either. But it's quite interesting knowing who's in charge.

[See The NEC of the ANC]

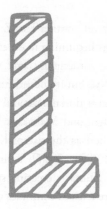

Laager mentality

A laager mentality should not be confused with a lager mentality. That is something entirely different and applies to the average South African male's attitude to what drink should accompany the watching of a sporting event. South African Breweries approves of a lager mentality.

No, a laager mentality with two As has nothing to do with beer; it has to do with a laager obviously, a term derived via the Dutch word for "camp" from the Trekboers' proclivity for making encampents by positioning their wagons in a defensive circle. This was to protect against the untrammelled dangers of the African night, be it wild beasts or wild darkies lurking with spears.

Today, an army platoon might park its armoured cars in a laager while on overnight patrol, and even a basic camping setup with the tents on the outside and a fire in the middle follows this pattern.

Key to the concept is the defensive circle protecting the vulnerable people within from the many threats outside. Equally important is that, once within the laager, where the fire is warm and illuminating and you can see all the pretty things you own, the outside world appears even darker and scarier than before and you vow to your fellows around you that you must protect each other no matter what to your dying breath. And so you come to the notion of a laager mentality. Which is what the apartheid government had back in the day, and was the reason why we ended up with an arsenal of nuclear weapons in the late '70s and early '80s. Because *they* were coming to get us.

Today the laager mentality is no longer confined to Trekboer pioneers and apartheid generals; it is ingrained in many of us and goes hand in hand with 20-foot perimeter walls, the success of the electric-fence industry and white people's attitude to queuing.

[See **Queuing**]

The leaf-blower problem behaviour / patterns

The leaf blower, heinous invention that it is, is a First World solution to a First World problem. How do you relocate leaves from one side of the garden to the other with a minimum of physical exertion while satisfying the masculine primal DIY needs of the average middle-aged developed-nation man? With a leaf blower, of course.

In South Africa we don't need leaf blowers because our masculine primal needs are satisfied simply by surviving the drive to work in the morning. Plus we have gardeners. And yet there are leaf blowers here, adding their own brand of aggravation to the urban soundtrack of wailing car and house alarms, Doppler-shifting police sirens, barking dogs, grinding angle grinders, mating Egyptian geese, screeching guinea fowl, offensive hadedas… Why they are here is a modern mystery.

Lowveld sunsets

places / paradise

Kruger Park, sun going down, G&T in hand. Baobabs and acacias silhouetting to black, hazy purple hills in the distance, crystal stars emerging one at a time (and later by the hundred). Sounds of the night bush beginning: fiery-necked nightjar, scops owl, possibly a hyena whooping… Is there anything better?

The luminescent rise of SA's black diamonds

people / stereotypes

Anyone who thinks Thabo Mbeki was a hopeless president who brought nothing but ruin to the country clearly hasn't been to Khanyi Dhlomo's Luminance in Hyde Park. Luminance is wondrous, a "luxury and contemporary fashion and lifestyle department" that is filled with Tom Ford, Manolo Blahnik, Armani and every other designer label under the sun – as well as snazzily dressed black diamonds lapping it all up. These luminescent Luminance shoppers are the vanguard of the steadily growing black middle class and, whether or not you're a fan of yuppiedom, or you think that too few of them have too much money, black diamonds are the future of the country. The more, the better.

Thuli Madonsela

The Public Protector is a Chapter Nine institution with the authority to investigate any government entity for wrongdoing. As a means of keeping a check on the running of government, it is thus a very important office – and yet no-one really bothered about it before. This is because the guy in charge, Lawrence Mushwana, didn't do too much other than (effectively) referee the odd internal ANC dispute. Then in 2009 he was given a R7-million payout for his loyal service and moved over to the Human Rights Commission, where he became its chairman.

Enter a relatively unknown human-rights lawyer by the name of Thulisile Madonsela. She had been one of 11 technical experts who worked on the drafting of the Constitution 15 years before and now, suddenly, she was the public protector. So, who was she?

Take Julius Malema, Steve Hofmeyr and Lawrence Mushwana and combine them into one (very scary) person – then Thuli

Madonsela is the complete antithesis of that person. But few people knew this when she was made public protector and many would have expected more sitting-on-derrière thumb-twiddling from her rather than actual public protecting, as per the job description. Wow. What a breath of fresh, righteous air.

Fast-forward a few years and Public Works Minister Gwen Mahlangu-Nkabinde, Cooperative Governance Minister Sicelo Shiceka and National Police Commissioner Bheki Cele have all been fired on her recommendation. These are some seriously big names. As a result, Thuli Madonsela has become the one political appointment in the entire country who everyone loves and respects. Everyone, that is, being the taxpaying public – possibly not the incompetent and/or corrupt politicians she's bending over a barrel.

Think about it: you don't have to see the preposterous Bheki Cele on TV any more because of this woman. If anything deserves a medal and a promotion to general, it's that.

Mielies

food / staple

As any follower of *Madam And Eve* knows, there is a lady who walks the suburbs of Johannesburg most weekdays, trundling along with her trolley and shrieking in a sharp but sustained tone: *M-I-E-L-I-E-E-E-E-S!* She has made a living for years doing this, and the fact that she continues to push her trolley through the suburbs despite Granny Anderson's best catapult-assisted efforts is testament to the sheer popularity of the foodstuff she sells. What is it that makes mielies so popular? And why don't we call them corn or maize like the rest of the world?

Last things first. *Mielie* is a throwback to the time of Bartolomeu Dias and company; the early Portuguese explorers gave us the word, from their *milho* – which goes to show that our Porra culinary flavour goes far deeper and further back than Nando's and peri-peri prawns.

As for our mielie obsession, that's slightly more difficult to explain, though one thing is for sure: like sugar and fast food, it knows no cultural barrier in South Africa. Mielie meal is a southern African staple, the basis of mieliepap and putu. Samp is another favourite, popularised in the Xhosa dish *umngqusho* – samp and beans, often served with chakalaka and said to be Nelson Mandela's favourite. Or we eat them straight up – boiled, grilled or (NB: best way!) on the braai. Then there is the symbolism that comes with the mielie, with great harvests of the crop signalling prosperity and abundance.

Come to think of it, Granny Anderson gives the Mielie Lady a real hard time.

Minibus taxis behaviour / transport

In the South African minibus taxi, you have one of the great industrial cornerstones of our economy. These 16-seater vehicles are vital cogs in our system of production, shuttling 65 percent of South Africans to and from their places of work. How's that for a figure? *Two-thirds* of our workforce is reliant on minibus taxis. Despite their inherent value to our country, though, the ubiquitous Zola Budd* is the pariah of our roads.

The public distaste for minibus taxis may have something to do with the fact that their drivers – and, by extension, the taxis themselves – are responsible, by AA estimates, for around 70,000 accidents each year. This despite making up only 2 percent of the vehicles on our roads. Simply stated, they are horrendous, horrendous hazards, and they flout just about every road law – and some criminal laws – on a daily basis. Speeding, tailgating, sudden stopping, illegal lane changing and red-robot jumping are the foundation on which taxi driving is based. But there are many advancements on these stock manoeuvres, and our current favourite is the way several taxis will happily block a robot intersection during rush-hour traffic even though it's clear they won't make it across when the light turns red; this way, they make no forward progress themselves but they do manage to prevent all the cars crossing the intersection in the perpendicular direction from doing so…

Sorry, we got distracted there. What we're trying to say is that minibus taxis get something of a bad rap, considering that government-funded public transport is nonexistent in certain (most) areas of the country. And even where the state does subsidise transport it is often prohibitively expensive. Minibus taxis are not perfect and they add a special brand of mayhem to our roads, but when you don't have the Gautrain, MyCiti, Metrobus, Metrorail, SafeCab or Golden Arrow to call on, the only other option is to grit your teeth and tolerate the blaring strains of Whitney Houston. For tourists, taxis are an experience. For the rest of us – whether you're a maid schlepping an hour or more to work, or the madam waiting at the other end – they're a necessary evil.

* Following the release of a Brenda Fassie song named after our famous '80s middle-distance runner, taxis became known, for their speed, as Zola Budds.

"Mlungu"

Mlungu is a Zulu term for a white person, from *umlungu*, which describes the white foam that arrives from the sea. Elsewhere in Africa there are similar (though possibly etymologically different) terms – *mzungu, musungu, murungu* – and it's common practice for them to be decreed contemptuous or pejorative today by the politically correct guardians of offence-taking.

On the contrary, mlungu is a brilliant word. Soccer player Dean Furman, sometimes the only white player in the Bafana Bafana squad, is met with passionate cries of *Mlunguuuu!* when he gets the ball and he's happy enough with it. And if a whiteboy wears his MLUNGU T-shirt out he's more likely to be met with smiles and friendliness from his black brethren than any kind of unkind tittering. If anything, it's something of an icebreaker. So embrace your inner mlunguness next time you're out on the town. (Assuming you're an mlungu, that is.)

"Moer, donner, bliksem"

To *moer, donner* or *bliksem* a person is to perpetrate an act of violence against that person, usually with your bare hands. In other words, to beat him up. So if someone says they want to moer, donner or bliksem you, you better be a) bigger than that someone, b) faster than him, or c) able to persuade him otherwise.

These three verbs are further examples of wonderfully evocative Afrikaans words that, for all their thuggish connotations, South African English can't do without. Moer is probably the more obscure of the lot, and in this sense it's possibly from *moor*, to murder. But you can also be the moer in, which means extremely angry and seems somehow to be derived from the Afrikaans for mother... The other two are more obvious derivations of the Dutch terms for thunder and lightning – so when you threaten to donner and/or bliksem someone you are, technically, implying that you'll be laying the smack down Zeus-style. Bliksem, however, has far wider interpretations; it can be used as an expletive (*Bliksem!*), as a noun to describe a bastard (*You bloody bliksem!* *angry*) or, as so often happens, the complete opposite (*You bloody bliksem!* *stoked*).

So. You're the moer in with someone? Go donner that bliksem.

Aaron Motsoaledi people / politics

If you ever get your hands on the book *SA Politics Unspun* by Stephen Grootes, in which 50 of the most important political players in the country are rated by the power and moral authority they wield, you'll find that only one of them gets a perfect 10 for the latter. That's Minister of Health Aaron Motsoaledi. This is because he is a gem: a hardworking, caring, hugely competent minister who's got one of the toughest jobs in the country and is performing like a champion. His track record in the battle against Aids alone is enough to warrant sainthood; from the dark days of Manto Tshabalala-Msimang we are now the epitome of global best practice, and our life expectancy has leapt under his watch.

Add in Motsoaledi's power rating of 7 and he's the highest-rated person in Grootes's book. Could we please have this type of guy in charge of every department in government? (But see **Lulu Xingwana** for the other end of the scale...)

The national bird of South Africa

animals / heritage

Officially, it's the blue crane, a tall, good-looking bird that you may spot standing regally alongside its mate in a farmer's field as you take a drive through the Western Cape interior.

Unofficially, it is the hadeda ibis, which is, quite clearly, the spawn of Satan in flying form. Unlike blue cranes, you'll probably see these vile creatures every day of your life because they are now *everywhere*, having spread from golf courses to playing fields to housing estates in the past couple of decades so that, like airborne vermin, they infest every nook and cranny in the land. More to the point, you'll most definitely hear them because they have the most distinctive, god-awful call under the sun, a screeching banshee wail they emit at all hours of the day and night that will rouse you (and your newborn child) from the deepest slumber to wide-eyed panicky wakefulness like a pinkie in your botty.

The NEC of the ANC
– and the reality of SA power

You know why South African politics is so confusing? Besides the fact that it's politics, that is? Because of the acronyms. Start with ANC, SACP, DA, IFP, NFP, ACDP, EFF, FF+, UDM – and you've only got the major political parties. By the time you get to the parastatals, trade unions and Chapter Nines it's like you're playing Scrabble. CONSAWU. SACCOLA. CPPRCRLC. Damn, I took one letter too many...

Here's a tip. If you want to narrow down what's important in the political news, look out for this selection of capital letters: ANC's NEC. That's the ANC's* National Executive Committee, the group of the top 80 or so members of the party, headed by Jacob Zuma and corralled by Gwede Mantashe, which meets every couple of months to make all the decisions that count, from whether to serve Cristal or Dom at the next anniversary celebration to what direction governmental policy will take. It's the core of South African political power, the acronym that matters.

* If you don't know that ANC stands for the African National Congress, then welcome to Earth, Mr Martian, have a nice stay.

Nkandla

Nkandla, as we all know, is Jacob Zuma's home in rural KwaZulu-Natal, and it has been the centre of rather a lot of controversy since it was reported in October 2012 that taxpayer money had been used to fund "security upgrades" there to the tune of R200+

million. But what exactly is Nkandla and what does the way you choose to describe it say about you?

If you think Nkandla is a homestead then you most likely enjoy Western movies and are possibly a racist.

If you think Nkandla is a compound then you are Helen Zille or someone else in a blue T-shirt looking for publicity, and you're definitely a racist who likes to use "language loaded with prejudice" (thanks for the insight, Mac Maharaj).

If you think Nkandla is Zuma's residence then you work for the SABC.

If you think Nkandla is a fortified country estate then you are a *New York Times* reporter who chooses his words carefully.

If you think Nkandla is a presidential palace then you're probably getting a little bit carried away with the whole thing and you may well be a troll on News24.

And if you think Nkandla is paid for entirely by Jacob Zuma and his family then there is a strong chance you believe in unicorns and the tokoloshe. At the very least, you've never had to apply for a home loan.

"Now", "now now" & "just now"

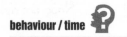

behaviour / time

None of these terms mean now. So, a guide:

"I'll be there now" = I am on my way and will be there shortly.

"I'll be there now now" = I intend to be there shortly, just got a little something to do in the meantime. Be patient.

"I'll be there just now" = Honestly, just stop bugging me. I'll be there when I'm there. If I feel like it.

But it really depends on your tone…

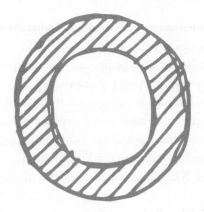

Okes, chinas & boytjies

You can talk about your okes or your chinas – as in, *Hey babe, me and the okes/chinas are going for a dop.* And you can call someone your china or your boytjie – as in, *Hey my china/boytjie, you wanna go for a dop?* But you don't call someone an oke or talk about your boytjies.

Hey oke, you coming for a dop?

Hey babe, the boytjies want to go for a dop.

Nope, not right. Doesn't work like that.

Other cities in SA (that aren't the up-their-own-arses Big Three) places / cities

You may have noticed elsewhere in these pages that there are individual entries for Johannesburg, Cape Town and Durban. This is a clear reflection of yet another inherent prejudice that underscores

South African life: that these are the only cities that "count".

Open any mainstream magazine and any time you come across advice that is supposedly for national consumption – whether it's new restaurants or bars, fashion stockists, medical specialists listed at the end of an article, anything – the magazine in question will offer several options in Joburg and Cape Town and one or two in Durban. That's it. Because, they figure, Pretoria is basically Joburg anyway and if you're going to add Bloem then you have to add PE and East London too, and probably Pietermaritzburg (Jesus, really?), and maybe even Kimberley, but then again the readers are more likely to be in Plett or Knysna than those places…

Long story short, Joburg, Cape Town and Durbs are the big guns. But while these cities may have the cream of the country's high-income urban population, we think this is an injustice. An outrage, even! So here's a line on each of those other places.

Pretoria: also known as Tshwane; administrative capital of South Africa; if you really have to visit then take the Gautrain because traffic from Sandton is a real nightmare.

Port Elizabeth: also known as the Windy City; windy.

East London: also known as Slummies; once voted the dodgiest city in the country; probably a fair call.

Bloemfontein: judicial capital of the country; place to stop when driving from Joburg to Cape Town. (Although, let's be honest, Colesberg is probably better.)

Kimberley: historically interesting diamond capital of the world; reason why South Africa started attracting attention to itself in the second half of the 19th century; home of the Big Hole, mined from 1871 until 1914; not much has happened there since.

Plettenberg Bay: long-time, well-deserved reputation for being Joburgers' second home and favoured destination for drunken teenagers celebrating matric rage; best beaches and weather in the world; pretty good if you can avoid the crowds.

Knysna: vies with Hermanus for the greatest transformation in the past three decades from sleepy, beautiful holiday village to commercially molested suburb-by-the-sea.

Pietermaritzburg: town near Durban.

Orlando Pirates v Kaizer Chiefs

In the apartheid days we didn't play international soccer. Then suddenly we did, and for a brief period, with Lucas Radebe, Doctor Khumalo and co, Bafana Bafana were wonderful. We won the African Cup of Nations, we qualified for the World Cup, we were competitive and proud... But for the last decade and more we've been appalling, with overpaid, underperforming foreign coaches unable to get Benni McCarthy to lose weight, let alone win games. (Now, at least, we have a local in charge, Gordon Igesund.)

So what do our soccer supporters really get worked up about? That would be Orlando Pirates versus Kaizer Chiefs, the South African El Clásico, a game that captures the imagination of fans from Cape Town to Musina even though their home stadiums are less than ten kilometres apart, in Soweto. Battle lines are drawn; vuvuzelas and makarapas (extravagantly decorated hard hats) are adorned with team symbols and colours; households become divided, with spouses even known to take opposing sides – during the game one might support the Buccaneers while the other is a Glamour Boy and so they must be bitter enemies... You don't need Bafana when you have the Sowetan derby.

Petrol attendants

people / stereotypes

Did you know that you may not legally open a self-service petrol station in South Africa? Officially, this is a measure of protection for petrol attendants, to preserve their jobs. Unofficially, it's because South Africans who aren't petrol attendants don't actually know how to put petrol in a car. Seriously. Have you tried it?

Political Come on-s!

politics / controversy

There is, it seems, no shame left when it comes to Zuma-era politics. Whatsoever. It's not like we didn't have the shenanigans and the hypocrisy and the self-serving agendas in the past, but there was a time when our politicians at least tried to maintain appearances. You know, tried not to make it so extraordinarily obvious. These days you can barely open a newspaper without shaking your head and thinking, *Really? Do they take us for such fools? Come on.*

Some highlights from the past few years:

In 2006 Schabir Shaik, Jacob Zuma's friend and financial advisor, was sentenced to 15 years in jail for corruption. He spent most of the next two years eating takeout in hospital before being granted medical parole because of his impending death due to some or other mystery illness. Five years later his death is still pending and in the meantime he likes to play golf, attend mosque regularly and tell news reporters how unfair it was that he had to go to jail... *Come on.*

In 2008 Hitachi Power Africa was awarded a multibillion-rand deal to provide boilers for Eskom's Medupi power station. Meanwhile, the ANC's investment company Chancellor House had a 25 percent stake in Hitachi and stood to make an estimated R1 billion in profit from the deal. And it just so happened that Eskom's chairman back then, Valli Moosa, was a member of the ANC's fundraising committee... *Come on!*

In 2009 Blade Nzimande was appointed Minister of Higher Education. At the same time, Nzimande was also the secretary-general of the South African Communist Party – as in a party for communists* – and yet within months of taking up his new role he was driving around in two government-funded BMW limousines that cost more than R1 million each... *Come on!*

In 2012 it was announced that Zuma's personal residence / compound / fortified country estate in Nkandla in rural KwaZulu-Natal had received "security upgrades" to the amount of R206 million – on the taxpayer's account. Zuma professes not to know a thing about it and the people at the Department of Public Works are wondering how on earth ~~the bloody public found out~~ the costs have escalated so astonishingly... *Seriously?! Come on!*

In 2013, the Gupta brothers launched ANN7, their 24-hour

news channel which, it was claimed, was not "pushing someone's agenda". The Guptas are friends with Zuma, his son is an investor in the station and Zuma visited the studio two days before the channel launched... *I mean, come on!*

Is this different to the politics that happens anywhere else in the world? No, probably not.

But come on!

* I know, communists – come on, right?

Poolitics

Politics is a realm of confrontation and hostility. Of arguments and counter-arguments. Of tussles, quarrels and squabbles. Of dust-ups and showdowns. Of bunfights, catfights and poo fights... Poo fights? Really? Oh yes, poo fights.

Politics is one thing, but *our* politics is another thing altogether. Anything goes. Shame is a thing of the past. See the entry right above for the evidence. Even when you've been found out at the highest level, fired as a cabinet minister and rebuked by Parliament, as happened to former Communications Minister Dina Pule in August 2013 due to a case of glaring nepotism, there appears to be no need to demonstrate contrition. "If I made a mistake, I want to apologise," Pule declared on receiving the maximum permissible fine from Parliament, presumably thinking no mistake had been made. It's a common attitude these days.

Still, her behaviour is nothing compared to the "affiliates" of the ANC Youth League who, protesting the standards of sanitation delivery to low-income houses in Cape Town, decided to voice their displeasure in the winter of 2013 by using the city as a broad canvas to paint with human excrement... As a means of drawing attention to yourself and your cause, throwing poo has its benefits. It gets you newspaper headlines, that's for sure – especially when you phone ahead to make sure the photographers will be there when you arrive at the airport or Western Cape legislature. But it also, one might think, detracts from your moral authority as someone who legitimately deserves to be heard. On anything. Ever.

Because you were throwing poo.

[See "**Kak**"]

Pronking

language / vocab

Dwaal, gatvol, kak... we've already come across a number of Afrikaans words that have been assimilated into South African English, but there are several that are now part of world English, full stop, and as a result don't even warrant their own vocab entries here. Veld (veldt), spoor, trek, commando and apartheid are examples; everyone knows what they mean. Two of them even made it into major Hollywood movie titles.*

Pronking, however, makes it in here because a) it's a little more obscure than the others, and b) it's just about the coolest of the lot, a word to describe the way a springbok jumps high into the air with its back arched and all four legs extended when threatened. It's a curious (and endearing) behaviour that has never been conclusively explained, because it requires a lot of energy and tends to direct the animal in question upwards rather than away from whatever is threatening it, almost as though it's putting on a show. One explanation is that the springbok is basically saying to the cheetah / wild dog / passing car *I see you there and I'm so totally awesome I can jump up and down on the spot here instead of running away, so really there is no point in chasing me and sorry for you.* It's this sense for which it's named: *pronk* literally means show off in Afrikaans, from the Dutch *pronken*, to strut.

Though they're the experts, it's not only springboks that pronk. Various types of gazelle are down with pronking, as are lambs and other young livestock, and some dogs – most hilariously of all, fox terriers, when chasing birds and mice in long grass.

* Star Trek and Commando, if you didn't work it out.

Protea problems

sport / tragedies

You may be wondering what, exactly, this little entry refers to – so let's clarify things right away. No, it's got nothing to do with fynbos. Yes, it's all about cricket.

If we'd slipped the word *choking* in there between *Protea* and *problems* the cricketing nature of this topic would have been evident from the start – but besides stepping on the toes of our nice little alliteration there, it also wouldn't speak to the truth of the matter. Because every time the Proteas lose their mettle in a major tournament, the C-word rears its head like a politician's illegitimate child – but the Proteas are *not* chokers. Unfortunately, it's now gone far, far deeper than that.

It is undeniable that our national cricket team has choked in the past. Take the World Cup 2011 quarterfinal, South Africa versus New Zealand in Mirpur, as an example. We have beaten the Black

Caps eight games out of the last ten. We are ranked above them, we are favoured to beat them, on paper we are superior to them, we are in good form in the tournament... Potential choke factors abound. Then we bowl well and restrict them to a sub-par score of 221. And an hour or two later we are cantering to victory at 108 for 2 on a nothing-much pitch without a worry in the world... At this point – and only at this point – are all the conditions for a genuine choke met. We are dominant, the win is in sight, literally the only way we can lose this match is by choking.

And lo, it came to pass.

A good outfield catch to a lazy shot gets us to three wickets down and that's it. Then comes the pushing and the prodding and the hesitating, with the tension rising and the eyes widening and the claustrophobia descending – and next thing we're 172 all out. That, my friends, is a choke.

But all the C-talk that has emerged over the years, as we fail miserably World Cup after ICC Championship after World Cup, tends to simplify a problem that is not that simple.

Famously – tragically, unforgettably – we tied the semi-final of the 1999 World Cup in Birmingham, and in so doing were knocked out of the competition on the merest of run-rate technicalities. But a game that was subsequently voted the greatest ODI of all time* was hardly a choke. It was a humdinger, a roller coaster, a titanic match between two excellent and evenly matched teams that just so happened to end in the most perfectly complete disaster (for us). Within the space of four balls we had virtually lost the game then (4, 4) virtually won the game then (near runout) nearly tied the game then (runout) tied the game. That's not a choke; it's two balls of adrenalised mayhem in a game filled with the stuff, is what that is.

As for the 2003 World Cup debacle in the Durban rain, another heart-breaking, competition-ending tie, with Mark Boucher purposefully blocking what was to be the last ball of the match, that too was no choke. It was a sportsman doing maths. It was a clerical error. The guys in the middle had got it spot on. And speaking of rain, let's take it all the way back to 22 March 1992 to the World Cup semi-final in Sydney that started it all. Going into the match as underdogs, the Proteas scrambled and scrapped their way to within reaching distance of England. But, as the rain gently fell for 12 minutes, the collective hope of a South African victory vanished on the back of the most inane technical ruling in history – never mind that the clouds parted and there was the rest of the night to finish the game. In that match the fates that had lofted team South Africa into the position of genuine World Cup contenders mercilessly tossed them aside as discarded also-rans – and it has been a script that has played out, in one form or another, at every major knockout tournament ever since, bar one. (The 1998 ICC Champions Trophy. No, I don't remember it either.)

Have the events that conspired to ruin our first big tournament come to do death to them all? Perhaps. But the type of death varies; it's not all choking. Choking is going down 8-9 in the America's Cup having been 8-1 up (Team New Zealand, 2013); or throwing away a three-shot lead on the 72nd hole at The Open (Jean van de Velde, 1999); or being 6-2, 6-4, 5-1 (30-0) up in a Wimbledon semi and then losing in five sets (Bill Tilden, 1927).

Yes, the Proteas choke – but we do so much more than that. We also panic and we self-destruct and we overthink and we underthink and we kotch on ourselves and we get rained on by the weather gods and screwed over by technicalities and, occasionally, we simply lose to a better team on the day. Potato, tomato, you may say. But it's important to differentiate these things because it brings rational sense to an otherwise mystical aberration.

So in summary, I say we're cursed. Makes it easier to process.

Meanwhile, for all the protean angst and disappointment that ODI cricket seems to dish up, South Africa remains king of the hill in the one version of cricket that hasn't yet been ruined by the era of modern professionalism: Test cricket.** As of October 2013 our team is, on paper, rather a little bit devastating. In Hashim Amla and AB de Villiers we have two of the top-three ranked batsmen in the world (and two of the most entertaining to watch); in Dale Steyn and Vernon Philander we have the two top-ranked bowlers, with the former having been at number one for four straight years; and in Jacques Kallis, we have one of the top players *of all time*. Overall, we are, happily, the top-ranked side by an enormous 15 percent margin.

And yet in this golden age of South African Test cricket, the Proteas had played just 24 matches in the ranking cycle to October 2013, compared to the 30 of India, 33 of Australia and 38 of England. This is, of course, our greatest cricketing problem – that we're not shining while we can. So before they turn Test cricket into a World Cup knockout tournament, I humbly suggest we play fewer limited-overs games and more Tests.

Thank you.

* Happily, a later South Africa-Australia game subsequently assumed that spot, the 438 match at the Wanderers in 2006. This was the Proteas' finest hour in ODI cricket, and was the diametric opposite of a choke.

** Is it the only version of the only game that hasn't been ruined by the era of modern professionalism? Quite possibly.

Queuing (an issue of personal space and land expropriation)

Unlike Poms, who queue for fun, South Africans need some guidance. Primarily it's this: if the person in front of you in the queue takes a step forward, this is not an invitation to try to enter him or her from behind.

Admittedly, we're talking mostly from a white person's point of view here – specifically a white woman queuing to pick up her Computicket reservations at Shoprite – and it's basically an issue of personal space. White South Africans, as we all know, are craven capitalists and are thus obsessed with the notion of private property that is theirs and theirs alone, and black people aren't allowed to just come in and take it. Hence the zone – or land, if you will – immediately surrounding them while they are waiting in the queue at Shoprite is their private, personal space which they've worked very hard for over the years, and no-one else should be allowed on it.

In an ideal world, a white person's personal space zone would extend to a radius of approximately five metres, be demarcated with an electric fence and include within it a large Rottweiler to make sure no-one gains access unlawfully. Realistically, though, Vanessa in Shoprite would be happy to not feel anyone's actual body warmth at any stage of the queuing process. She would also prefer it if the maids in her neighbourhood didn't have shouting conversations across the street at 7am.

Black people, meanwhile, are great sharers of things and they also travel frequently in minibus taxis, often with up to six people in a row; they worry about other things.

The race card

As with so many polarised issues these days, racism – and the race card – is so very often seen in black and white. As in "That's racist!" rather than, "That's insensitive, or offensive, or annoying, or potentially hurtful" or even "I disagree with what you're saying".

Look, everyone, the AWB is racist. Julius Malema is racist. The people who suggest that VIP police officers drive too quickly or that Sylvia Lucas spent too much money on fast food or that affirmative action has its merits are not racist because of what they're suggesting. Which is not to say that they aren't immune to criticism or have an attitude problem, either; that may or may not be the case. And that's just another element of the problem. Because the race card – in this type of case, a reaction to a criticism – is a double whammy. First, it refuses to acknowledge the initial criticism in any meaningful form and so prevents any self-examination, then it automatically prevents the criticiser from examining his own argument or assumptions, which are quite possibly flawed. There is no engagement; positions are entrenched; battle lines deepen. Eventually you reach a situation where everyone is shouting and no-one is listening. Such is the argumentative, hyperbolic way of the modern world.

The thing is, race and racism are undeniable in South Africa. They're massive. They lurk. We can't not deal with them. Like the Jew card in the US – as Albert Brooks has joked – the race card never expires in SA. It will be with us always and, as such, it needs to be used wisely: a hammer blow to the vindictive and small-minded, not a knee jerk to the slightest provocation.

Here endeth the lesson.

Cyril Ramaphosa

people / politics

He really should be our next president. But it just seems so far away.

[See **Nkosazana Dlamini-Zuma**]

Robot hawkers

people / nuisances

One of the downsides of living where we do, at the very bottom of the Dark Continent, where the harsh realities of day-to-day living and the contemplations of which route to the beach to take tend to stay front of mind, is that we are, as a rule, technologically backwards. Television, for example, has been the most important media tool in the Western world since the '50s, but was only introduced to South Africa more than two decades later. The iTunes Store has been selling digital music to Americans since 2003 and has been the world's biggest music vendor since 2010, but South Africa only caught up in 2013. The global average internet download speed is currently around 14MB/s, but we trundle along, infuriatingly, at less than 4MB/s. And a lot of us still think BlackBerrys are the business. (Wake up, people! You may as well have a hand-crank telephone in your bag.)

Point being that, when the incredible notion of electronically controlled traffic signals, with green, orange and red lights, was introduced to South Africa in the 1930s, to replace the policemen who manually guided traffic at road intersections, this was seen as revolutionary. "Traffic lights" would hardly do as a descriptive term for these futuristic robot policemen, though...

And so, to this day, we are the only country in the world with traffic that is controlled by "robots".

And though we may not be the only country where people hawk their wares at robots, we must surely possess some of the most innovative, entrepreneurial, diverse, opportunistic and utterly bloody annoying vendors of goods and services at road intersections – otherwise known as robot hawkers – in the world.

In the not-too-distant past South African drivers enjoyed the convenience of being able to buy their morning newspaper on the way to work without leaving the comfort of their cars. This was because they were sold at traffic lights. Nowadays, a driver can stock up on so much more at your average set of robots: cellphone chargers, refuse bags, shoe holders, colourful paintings, plastic hangers, plastic toys, inflatable globes, multi-coloured children's windmills, wooden carvings, a wide variety of fruit, flowers and cooldrinks, home-made jewellery, licence-disc holders, beaded wire animals, aircraft and other creations, pirated DVDs, and the inevitable collection of knock-off sports shirts and jerseys. He will be asked to provide small change in exchange for photocopied pages of lame jokes, or for one of two possible cleaning services: the first entailing general car litter being emptied into the hawker's proffered black bag (and then thrown over the wall into some guy's garden when the bag gets full), and the second involving unsolicited street kids pouring dirty water on his windscreen and then rubbing it off, with no discernible BEFORE and AFTER difference. And, of course, there will be an assortment of beggars and chancers, crippled by their addictions and/or physical handicaps, who offer nothing but their outstretched hands.

For many middle-class South Africans who prefer their informal economies out of sight and out of mind, negotiating the robots on the way to work in the morning has become a quite stressful event. Windows up, no eye contact, knuckles whitening on the steering wheel... Or you can try to roll with it and say things like "Hayibo!" and "Sharp sharp!" while grinning stupidly and waiting for the lights to change.

At least buy *The Big Issue*, from time to time.

The rooi gevaar, updated for the 21st century

politics / theory

rooi gevaar *n.* red danger [directly from Afrikaans], specifically the threat that the communist movement within Africa posed to South Africa during the apartheid years; the Nationalist government's greatest fear (after the swart gevaar obviously)

As world philosophies go, communism has not been a winner. The Russians got it wrong. So did the Chinese. We're not being unkind or anything; it's how it is. Stalin, Pol Pot, Mao Zedong – these are not model standard bearers for a happy system of social organisation. The result of the Cold War – USA 1: Soviet Union 0 – was similarly problematic. In summary, communism was a policy that, during its heyday, produced widespread economic ruin from the cold soulless factories of Eastern Europe to the warm soulless factories of the Southeast Asian jungle. It produced famine and hardship. It produced tyranny and people with sad faces. About the only good thing communism produced was *Animal Farm* by George Orwell.

Most importantly, for our purposes, this is not news. Look up communism in the dictionary and it will say something about classless societies and shared means of production and that it's bad, mkay. It may even call it the worst mistake of the 20th century.

So, about those communists in our government then…

Given what we know about communism – that is, it doesn't work – it can be a little disconcerting to mull too long over the fact that Blade Nzimande (Higher Education), Rob Davies (Trade and Industry), Yunus Carrim (Communications), Thulas Nxesi (Public Works) and Lechesa Tsenoli (Cooperative Governance and Traditional Affairs) are all cabinet ministers in the South African government as well as members of the SACP. As in the South African Communist Party. And, even more disconcerting, that the SACP still exists and in fact makes up one third of the Tripartite Alliance, the political entity that supposedly guides South Africa's governing policies.

How is their thinking relevant to South Africa in a world that has shunned the policy that they base their thinking on? The obvious answer is, it isn't. But because of the history of liberation in South Africa, in which the SACP played an undeniably important role, we now have communists in senior positions of government.

If you're an old Nat who looks fondly on days long gone, this may be your worst nightmare. Bloody reds in charge! After all, this is why we went to all that effort to build our own nuclear bombs back in the '70s. Just in case those Russian-backed commie bastards ever made it to our doorstep…

Time to take a deep breath, everyone. Because our communists aren't really communists. They just like to pretend they are. They're actually faux-ironic communists because faux irony is the in thing nowadays, like growing a mullet, lamb chops and a moustache or wearing a Hawaiian shirt. It used to be cool but now it's uncool although actually it's cool again because it gets you the attention you're looking for.

So, you see, this is how Nzimande, the general secretary of the SACP, can get away with driving a million-rand BMW (which is of course owned by the citizens of the country, not him). Or how Gwede Mantashe, one of the most powerful people in the country, can punt one economic policy as secretary-general of the ANC and another one entirely as chairman of the SACP. As for the distinct possibility that South Africa will have a Russian-built nuclear reactor costing a trillion rand or more – with all the corruptive opportunities that this cosy little setup presents – built at Pearly Beach or somewhere similar on the south coast in the next five to ten years, well, that's got faux irony written all over it…

The real problem is the trade unionists. Not only do they believe all that Marxist, capitalism-is-the-devil, hard-left mumbo-jumbo, they have some serious political power too.

[See **Laager mentality** and **The Tripartite Alliance**]

Shark-cage diving

animals / controversy

Every couple of years there is a spate of great white shark attacks, invariably in False Bay or along the south coast, that ignites the long-running shark-cage diving debate. It's not quite fracking (see **The fracking Karoo**), but it certainly raises temperatures, which is no surprise given that we're talking about encounters with the definitive monster of our primal nightmares.

Shark-cage diving habituates sharks to human activities and encourages them to associate humans with food, goes the one argument. Rubbish, goes the other; if sharks had become accustomed to eating us there would be *Jaws* scenes playing out on a daily basis at Fish Hoek and Muizenberg during summer. Without sufficient scientific data – or even a proper notion of how we would acquire such data – there seems to be no way to definitively prove who is or isn't right. So cage diving continues – and it's likely to do so for the foreseeable future. Because while the pro-cage-diving industry clearly has its own vested interests to consider when defending its side of the argument, there is one factor that will keep 99.9 percent of anyone who's ever cage dived on their side too: it is such a profoundly, overwhelmingly radical experience.

I mean, it's Jaws, the definitive monster of your primal nightmares, remember? And he's an arm's-length away from you.

Fuck me.

Springbok madness
(a.k.a. Bok befok)

sport / fans

Bok is a shortening of the word Springbok, and the Springboks are the South African rugby team. *Befok* (literally befucked) means crazy or even crazily good. So Bok befok describes the craziest, most worked-up, most hyper, most excited, most obsessed, most loyally one-eyed Springbok fans out there. Which is basically all of them.

How, you ask, does Bok befok manifest itself? It manifests itself in grown men and women buying R750 technofabric Springbok supporters' jerseys and wearing them to work on Bok Friday (otherwise known as Bokday). And in sold-out tour packages to follow the Springboks playing in freezing-cold, rain-soaked Cardiff and Scotland in the dead of northern hemisphere winter. In people thinking *Die Leeuloop* was cool. In Pieter de Villiers getting guest-speaker invites. In watermelon hats. In customised green bakkies adorned in springbok motifs and with BOK BEFOK stencilled on the windscreen. Literally stencilled in capitals on the front windscreen (which is, among other things, illegal).

And in less wonderful ways, Bok befok manifests itself in referees Bryce Lawrence and Romain Poite fearing for their lives should they ever come to South Africa after blundering major Test matches, and, most notoriously, in the grossly overweight, booze-fuelled spectator Pieter van Zyl tackling referee David McHugh mid-match in Durban in 2002. Not great PR for South Africa, that particular incident…

It may be interesting to note that there are some South African rugby fans who are more befok than Bok fans; they're called Blue Bulls supporters and they're known to have Blue-Bulls-themed weddings (say no more). And note also that not *all* South African rugby fans are Bok befok. Some conscientious sports objectors who didn't support our national teams during the apartheid years and still hold a grudge 20 years later publicly cheer for our nemesis team, the All Blacks, by painting their faces black and wearing All Black paraphernalia when they play in South Africa. This makes Bok fans even more Bok befok.

Strike season

behaviour / patterns

In South Africa there is a "season" for strikes. This notion alone is problematic for any capitalist pig dog contemplating it. But then you consider that strike season usually peaks in July and August, months that correlate quite closely with the absolute middle of winter, a period when reliable employment and income would probably be more cherished than at any stage in the year. It just makes no sense. No sense at all.

Supermarkets

If anyone ever doubts the fact that apartheid still exists, a tour of his local supermarkets should disabuse him of the notion in short time. Because never is the concept of economic apartheid more prevalent than when we're shopping for our groceries. On the one side we have the hermetically sealed, industrially shrinkwrapped, perfectly coloured, beautifully labelled produce at Woolworths, with its SUV-driving soccer mom / black diamond clientele who enjoy making use of the antiseptic handwipes at the entrance and couldn't tell you how much they've just paid when they leave, and on the other we have Third World value for money and comparative chaos at Shoprite (or, more accurately, the township spaza shop). Pick n Pay and Checkers are somewhere in between and your local Spar could be at either end of the scale because they're all independently managed. Wherever you buy your cereal and loo paper, you've been classified.

The swart gevaar

If the rooi gevaar, or red danger, was the obsessive mental affliction that befell Nationalist Afrikaners during the 1960s and '70s (see **The rooi gevaar**), then the swart gevaar, or black danger, was the even more serious illness that affected them from the very first day they came into power in 1948. Those poor Nats just couldn't handle their reds or blacks. How they got their accounting done is anyone's guess.

Those who still suffer from the swart gevaar today tend to move to Perth and elsewhere.

[See **The great emigration debate**]

"T.I.A."

Short for "This is Africa" and, as such, our take on *c'est la vie* – except that rather than a Frenchman shrugging his shoulders because he's just found out his wife's sleeping with his neighbour, this is more likely a Saffer shaking his head because he's just paid a R50 bribe to get out of a R1,200 speeding ticket.

The tokoloshe

African mythology is rife with tales of mischievous, furry, well-endowed, hyper-sexual, dwarfish water sprites known as tokoloshes. Then again, so are the weekly South African tabloids. It's a sad day indeed when the headline TERROR OF THE GAY TOKOLOSHE! doesn't warrant your attention (*Daily Sun*, August 2012).

While there are those who dismiss, perhaps quite rationally, the existence of a strange, nocturnal leprechaun-cum-baboon-type creature who carries his sleeping victims off into the night, the superstitious practice of elevating one's bed using paint tins or bricks is remarkably common throughout South Africa – as is the tokoloshe's regular portrayal in our popular media. Music videos, song titles, cartoon strips, under your bed – the tokoloshe is everywhere…

Township tours

places / tourism

Township tours can vary a fair bit. They can be used by school history classes as an educational tool for highlighting the evils of apartheid, by Irish tourists to get inspired for their next community construction project, or by students keen to try drinking Black Label quarts in a shebeen. But there's really no way of getting around the fact that two things are happening here.

1. You, as the paying client, are boarding a bus to go look at poor people and see how they live.
2. Poor people are making money by showing tourists how they live.

It's exploitation squared, and if you live in South Africa or are just visiting you really should be part of it. Expect to see shacks in an astounding array of configurations, butchers on the side of the road selling sheep heads and all the rest, and a way of life that will make you think twice before complaining about the fluffiness of your soufflé or your intermittent WiFi signal. You'll also see homes that are proudly cared for, interiors that defy external appearances and a surprising number of satellite dishes.

The beauty of the township tour is that you can, as you board the bus with Sven from Sweden and Brittany from the USA, feel safe. Keep in mind, though, that unless you're going to sleep in a drafty tin shack, heat your water on a paraffin stove and curl up with eight members of your host family in a room smaller than the minibus you came in, you can't say you have really *experienced* a township. You're not going to be mugged while going to the outside loo and you're even less likely to witness a vigilante necklacing. But that shouldn't put you off going because there are lots of other interesting things to see in a township.

You will get some nice eats and a drink at the local shebeen. You might even be fortunate enough to taste a mopane worm (mmm, nutritious). You'll also have a peek at the local school where the children will sing you a song and then you'll visit a community project where you'll be shown exactly what kind of social upliftment is going on in the neighbourhood.

The assumption is that a township tour will leave you feeling just a little guilty if you happen to live above the poverty line. But the truth is that very few tours concentrate on the past; they are more concerned with showing you the various projects and possibilities for the future. Yes, it's a little voyeuristic – but it's voyeuristic in a responsible, non-exploitative way. Or, at least, in a responsible *co*-exploitative way. Either way, it shouldn't be only for tourists.

The Tripartite Alliance

After the unbanning of the liberation movements in 1990, the ANC formally joined forces with the SACP and Cosatu to form the Tripartite Alliance. These were three distinctly different political organisations, with their own constitutions and memberships, coming together to form one powerful entity to represent the people – the liberators, the communist left and the workers forging one political path together, a greater force than the sum of their parts. What could possibly go wrong?

What could possiblar go wrong?

Whet cold parssiblay gerring?

Wheat cod with parsley dressing?

Well, it may as well be. How do you make sense of it otherwise? Now into its third decade of existence, the Tripartite Alliance is effectively one half BEE capitalists, one half died-in-the-wool communists, and one half self-destructing, economically disastrous unionists. No, it doesn't quite add up, does it?

Wheat cod with parsley dressing, indeed.

[See The ANC, Strike season and The rooi gevaar]

Two-tone shirts

The venerable two-tone shirt is a utilitarian safari-type short-sleeved shirt, traditionally designed in khaki or a similarly earthy green or brown tone. The defining characteristic of the two-tone shirt is the thick trim on the twin breast pockets and the front seam that is rendered in a slightly darker khaki, green or brown tone. Hence the "two-tone" effect for which it is quite ingeniously named. For many South Africans, especially those with Dutch ancestry, a deep olive complexion and a love for the tilled soil, the two-tone shirt is a closet staple worn on a regular, if not daily, basis, and without which they would be sartorially all at sea.

A casual observer may spot the two-tone shirt and its wearer in the streets of any major South African city and at Springbok supporter events of any kind. For guaranteed sightings visit any Benoni, Springs or Durbanville shopping mall, and to witness the item worn at its proudest (and most appropriate) go hang around on a farm in the Free State. If you're lucky, the farmer – possibly Jan-Piet van Tonder whose wife made you a delicious lunch with sugared vegetables earlier – will be wearing astonishingly tight khaki short-shorts and khaki veldskoens* and he'll keep a comb in his long khaki socks.

Unsurprisingly, the Afrikaner man assumes responsibility for the two-tone shirt because of his inherent love for the outdoors combined with his generally practical nature and his total lack of any semblance of style whatsoever. You will find it stocked across the country in relatively upmarket stores that really should know better (ahem, Cape Union Mart), but please note that any ambitions you may have to eradicate from South African society the two-tone shirt should be met with reluctance. Attempts have already been made – with disastrous consequences. Witness the rise of two-tone jackets and fleeces, not to mention the *three*-tone shirt, a most appalling addition to the pantheon of utterly hideous South African fashion. In fact, the two-tone shirt and its three-tone offshoot are so gloriously disastrous that they have been embraced as an ironic uniform of sorts for bachelor parties, boys' fishing weekends and student theme parties across the land.

But wait! There's more!

The logical progression of two- and three-tone shirts? Yes, that would be two- and three-tone *houses*. Seriously. Next time you're cruising the northern suburbs of Cape Town or the southern and western suburbs of Johannesburg, check out the bright lilac or sky blue or burnt-orange houses with their off-white/cream/pale-yellow/beige window and door trimmings. There are entire two- and three-tone suburbs. It's madness. And mesmerising in its three-flying-ducks-on-a-wall way.

* **veldskoen** *n.* durable utilitarian shoe, traditionally made from animal hide and worn by Dutch settlers. Directly translated from Afrikaans as "field shoes", implying they should be worn in a field and nowhere else. Have, amazingly, become something of an international fashion trend in 2013 – which goes to show how moronic the fashion world is.

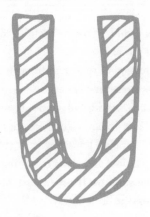

The (unavoidably confrontational) misinterpretation of struggle songs

politics / controversy

Jacob Zuma sang *Bring Me My Machine Gun* (*Awuleth' Umshini Wami*); Julius Malema (and others) sang *Shoot The Boer* (*Dubul' iBhunu*); anti-Zionist protesters sang *Shoot The Jew* (*Dubul' iJuda*) at a Jewish concert (in August 2013!) – and on each occasion people complained. Mostly white people.

The first one caused all sorts of trouble and strife when JZ used it to fire up his supporters back in the rape-trial days (these days he just listens to it on his iPod, presumably). The second one was found to be unconstitutional and led to Malema being convicted of hate speech. And this implies – not that you necessarily need to be told by an outside authority – that the third one is problematic too.

The thing is, we're informed, songs about shooting the boer/

Jew are not actually "about killing white people" (relief!); they're about identifying with the struggle, or a specific cause. When UCT historian Rebecca Hodes lamented the singing of *Shoot The Jew* and called it anti-Semitic, she was taken to task by one Tokelo Nhlapo, who describes himself as a social activist and core member of the Wits Palestinian Solidarity Committee.

"She clearly lacks an understanding of the spirit in which songs of the struggle are sung and her selective application of information and history shows her own ignorance and hypocrisy," Nhlapo wrote. The songs have symbolic value, those who sing them argue. They're not to be taken at face value.

At the same time, the songs are officially condemned by the powers that be to avoid any legal trouble (presumably). And yet the apologies are often qualified ("It's unfortunate but..."), suggesting that they may be a bit sorry, but they're not planning on doing much to prevent it happening again.

This, I'm afraid, is one of those poignant, uniquely South African points of conflict – invariably race-related – that no-one has an answer to and just about the best response is to shake your head, say eish, and change the topic.

Unimpeachable legends of South Africa

people / icons

No, Nelson Mandela is not a god. He is a complex human, with all that comes with it. Still, he's unimpeachably awesome – a description that probably applies to no other South African politicians (and not many world ones). But it also applies to these talented, genuine, all-round brilliant people:

Yvonne Chaka Chaka	Johnny Clegg
Hansie Cronje	Riaan Cruywagen
Ernie Els	Bryan Habana
Penny Heyns	Miriam Makeba
Hugh Masekela	Lucas Radebe
Desmond Tutu	Pieter-Dirk Uys

And, if we want to go back in time a bit, Sailor Malan.

If anyone has a bad word to say about them, you may flick them a bird that is officially endorsed by the people of South Africa.

But kidding about Hansie Cronje. He was a complete chop.

The unlawful police

politics / controversy

The roll call of high-profile South African policemen of recent times includes former national police commissioners Jackie Selebi (convicted felon) and Bheki Cele (fired for incompetence and/ or corruption), former head of police crime intelligence Richard Mdluli (on trial for murder, fraud, intimidation and other crimes) and former metro police chief Robert McBride (convicted of drunk driving and sentenced to jail for defeating the ends of justice). In August 2013 it was reported that nearly 1,448 police officers had been found to have criminal records in an audit dating to 2010. In October 2013 the Independent Police Investigative Directorate announced that it had had 7,628 cases of police brutality and criminality reported to it in the previous year.

That's tough to beat. No wonder political journalist Ranjeni Munusamy describes the position of national police commissioner as "the worst job in South Africa".

"Voetsek!"

Via Afrikaans from Dutch, where it translates as a shortening of "be off, I say". Suffice to say, voetsek (or voetsak) conveys a little more emotion than "be off, I say". Closer to eff off, more like.

Vuvuzelas

sport / annoyances

The unofficial symbol of the 2010 Soccer World Cup, the vuvuzela has been called an "instrument from hell", which is quite complimentary, really, given that the instrument tag implies some sort of melodic or rhythmic quality when all it produces is a monotonous drone akin to an apocalyptic swarm of bees. That said, freedom of expression is pretty important to us South Africans, so while some (most?) of us might decry the noise that the vuvuzela makes, we will defend to the death the right to make it.

Weather misconceptions weather / patterns

One of the privileges of being South African is the generally fantastic weather we're blessed with, and we love to lord it up over our friends and relatives in Canada and New Zealand and particularly in the UK – those poor suckers with their miserable perma-rain and their three-week summers…

But it's not like we have it all our way down here, as any Capetonian who's had a Gauteng immigrant harping on about the insufferable Cape winter knows. After ten minutes of *geez, it's been pouring all week* and *nooit, it was like gunfire in my ceiling* and *please guys, I just want to see the sun!*, you really do start feeling a bit insecure about the place. May as well live in Glasgow or the Isle of Skye, as far as the Vaalies are concerned. Well, screw you, Vaalies! With your tennis-ball hail stones and no-oxygen air and crisp, clear, always-beautiful July days…

Actually there are weather problems everywhere. Besides the

rose-ruining hail, the Highveld can get so dry that your lips peel off as you're disembarking at OR Tambo, while east-coast humidity makes the average KZN summer hellaciously unbearable (like the average Sharks fan). Meanwhile, the Karoo and Kalahari may get all the sun in the world – Upington is the fifth sunniest city in the world, apparently, and Bloemfontein's not too far behind – but it pays for this with the coldest of gonad-shrinking winter cold. And it never stops blowing from PE to East London…

Still, we've got it real good here weather-wise, and if you took a hypothetical year off to experience it at its best you could do worse than starting on the Garden Route in January, heading to Cape Town for February-May, then up to the KZN coast for the most magic winter imaginable, then over to Joburg (or the lowveld) for a sensational early summer, and back to the Garden Route.

Or just spend it all in Plettenberg Bay, which has, hands down, the best weather in the country. (NB: not Knysna.)

"Wena?" / "Jy?"

 language / vocab

When these words are used on their own, you might consider them the most abrupt, direct and impolite ways to greet anyone. Because in English, simply yelling "YOU?" at someone is usually considered offensive. Yet in some Zulu and Afrikaans circles, addressing someone – depending on the circumstances, naturally – with a quick "Wena?" and "Jy?" respectively, is widely accepted. We're not talking Jan-Piet on his Free State farm here; more like Galatia in Mitchell's Plain spotting the local skollies smoking outside her house. *"Jy? Hou op, julle fokken skelms!"* Come to think of it, sometimes it's quite impolite in Afrikaans, too.

Who's your bru, bro?
(And general surfer lingo)

Surfing is a pursuit based purely on fun. And you know what's not fun? School. Reading. Phonics. Vocabulary. Full sentences. Proper English. So, instead, surfers use their hands to describe their stoke, sometimes supplementing this with noises that sound as if their faces have just been punctured. Monosyllabic three-letter words are drawn out to form full sentences that speak volumes.

How was it?

Bruuuuuuuuuuuuuuuuuuuuu…

Which, depending on the hand signals, body language, inflection and enunciation employed, could mean anything from, "Very good, sir!" to "Really not good at all, my friend."

But then bru could also just as easily be bra or bro or breh or bruh or broseph or bullcat…The surf tribe is made up of numerous smaller tribes and in the same way that an Eskimo has 603 words for ice, the surfer has an equal number of words for his brethren.

And depending on the surfer's local break, he'll have his own geographical surf slang. For instance, Durbanites will say something like, *Aye, cuz, I'm still at my porzie but just now let's waai for wetties, do a bankie and grip a betty*. And while the Cape surfer will understand exactly what's being said, he will speak in a parlance of his own: *Nooit bru, you know I don't schmaak to skyf. Makes me too para. Gotta keep suss. But let's get some dops in and cruise some dollies. Aweh*. However, it's in between the South African coast's dimples where you get the most inbred surf slang; those guys who surf between the Kei and the Kowie specifically. 'Slunden, a.k.a. Slummies, has guys speaking as if they're gargling a mouth full of marbles. *Your arse is lank red, hey? Been choefing sut, or farting with the South Wester, broe?* Nobody knows what surfers in PE sound like because no surfer worth his Sex Wax has ever stuck around long enough to find out, so the closest they've ever been is probably Jeffreys Bay, where you'll be greeted with a friendly *Fokkof poes!*

And then it's all…

Yussis, but you okes are lank agro, hey?

What kind, ek sê? You don't just rock up here like it's your ma's porzie.

Oke, what's your plak? You schnaaid me dik on that last bomb.

Naught. How's your mind? I've been paddling for a wave since this arvie. I'm kished now. What a las.

I'm bleak, may broo. I've got you sussed.

Hey, choon me and I'll be bleak. I don't care if you've got lank connections. I've got my cuzzies, too.

You better just go home and doss tonight because if I see you at the jol it's ganna be hectic.

You'd better keep skay. I'm not skaam, hey. I'll moer you.

Is it?

Fully.

Kiff.

Hundreds.

Bruuuuuuuuuuuuuuuuuuu…

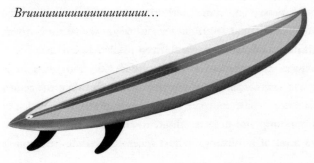

Lulu Xingwana

Earlier in the book we met Minister of Health Aaron Motsoaledi, the shining light of South African governance and the example we'd like other cabinet ministers to lead by. At the other end of the scale we have Lulu Xingwana, head of (deep breath) the Department of Women, Children and People with Disabilities – or DWCPD for short.

Lulu Xingwana is absolutely bloody hopeless. On Stephen Grootes's power and moral authority rating Motsoaledi scored 17 out of a possible 20. Lulu Xingwana got 4. By comparison, Marthinus van Schalkwyk got 8. Even Fikile Mbalula got 7.

Xingwana's inadequacies are multifaceted, both amazingly petty and extraordinarily damaging. She's the type of person who seems to court controversy intuitively, often on the back of an astoundingly misjudged comment, and then follows that up with a level of governing ineffectiveness to match. She's made the news for apparently ordering an expensive portable toilet for her personal use, for storming out of a photographic exhibition because there were pictures of naked lesbians on display, for making racist remarks about Afrikaners on international radio, and for overspending on furniture for her ministerial office. Not the right reasons to be making the news, it might be concluded.

As the most incompetent of politicians seem to do, she's managed to find her way into a number of departments; previously she headed up Agriculture and Land Development and then Arts and Culture. She also has the mandatory allegations of governing impropriety to her name that mark the truly compromised leader; in this case it was claims that she tried to interfere with certain deals with the Land Bank while at Agriculture.

But Xingwana's greatest failing is in her current position in charge of the new DWCPD. No doubt it is a department that by virtue of its name alone was doomed to failure – at one stage they were considering calling it the Department of Everyone Except Able-Bodied Men, as many observers joked at the time (because the joke was so bloody obvious), but that didn't roll off the tongue quite like the Department of Women, Children and People with Disabilities does. And yet Xingwana has managed to avoid meeting the most modest of expectations. In the spirit of Stella Sigcau, she has embraced the opportunity to make a real difference in an area that needs a real difference to be made, and she's done... bugger all. Or thereabouts. Here's a minister who should be in the news every day doing something about the greatest scourge in our society: violence against women and children. Instead, her department sends out press releases during August, the inane Women's Month, and then mires itself in inertia for the rest of the year. In three years since its inception the department has gobbled up R500 million and can point to no notable achievement.

In March 2013 the portfolio committee that monitors the DWCPD visited its offices. Among other things, it found that the place was a dump ("unsuitable and dirty"), there were insufficient computers and filing cabinets ("documents were stored in boxes and on piles on the floor") and the deputy minister's office was in another building. In its subsequent report it strongly implied that the department was providing false information to mislead Parliament about its achievements; at the very least, conflicting data suggested gross incompetence. Xingwana was described as "prone to have rage attacks when confronted with uncomfortable facts" and there were numerous cases of suspicious spending, including overpaid staff and huge severance payments.

To top it off, the light in the disabled toilet had apparently not worked for a year. That is, the disabled toilet at the Department of Women, Children and People with Disabilities… Honestly, even the Minister of Silly Walks could not make this shit up.

Xylophones (and marimbas) music / instruments ♫

How often can you legitimately use "xylophone" in an alphabetic list? Not often, that's how often. But we can here because marimbas, a kind of deep-toned xylophone, are popular enough in South Africa to justify a mention. Schools teach marimba classes. Minister in the Presidency Collins Chabane once played in a marimba band at the Oppikoppi Music Festival. Marimbas are cool.

Boom.

"Yebo" / "Ja" / "Ewe"

Hardly anyone in South Africa says yes any more. You say yebo (Zulu), ja (Afrikaans) or ewe (Xhosa). If you're trying to maintain the cool factor then you could try *yebo-yes*, and after *ja* you'll probably want to add a *bru* or a *boet*. Ja on its own can sound a bit gormless (or, oddly enough, a bit Brit toff). Ja boet. Ja bru. Ja well for sure. Those all work. Whatever you do, make sure you pronounce ewe as *e-we* (air-wear) not *ewe* (you)...

Youth unemployability

Downer alert!

Many people would argue that the biggest problem in South Africa is unemployment. With the figures somewhere between 25 percent (officially) and nearly 40 percent (unofficially), they'd have a good point, what with all our criminal and socioeconomic difficulties stemming from these particular stats. But the real biggest problem is not just unemployment; it's youth unemployment.

Every year 1.1 million young Saffers enter the labour market, but only 300,000 of them find formal employment. Nearly half of our 20-to-24-year-olds are officially unemployed – the unofficial figure is almost too scary to contemplate – and all the indicators see us way behind BRIC countries and other emerging-market nations. What's left over is millions of young people sitting around twiddling their thumbs and thinking of inventive ways to make ends meet – and not all of them will equate inventive ways with working hard to find an informal job... These are the young adults of today who've suffered the failed experiment of outcomes-based education, but who have been brought up on the expectation, even entitlement, of a brighter future. And no boss wants them because they are the unemployable future of our country.

So, you know, if you want to get down about something, no need to watch *Carte Blanche*, just think about that.

[See *Carte Blanche*-induced loser's syndrome]

"Yussis & jislaaik"

vocab / slang

Yussis, but that last topic wasn't so cool, hey? Unlike yussis, which is a totally cool word. Or yissis, or yasis. Whatever. Even jislaaik, which is where it comes from. Better than geez, at any rate. And not as rude as Jesus.

Zapiro

You may want to scream Aaaargh! when you read the headlines (see **Aaaargh!**), but there's still at least one good reason to buy the newspaper: Zapiro.

Helen Zille - a vision of a women-led future?

It's taken a woman to turn the Democratic Alliance into the formidable opposition force it is today. Under Helen Zille's sometimes frightening watch, the party took control of the Western Cape in 2009, ramped up its performance at the national elections at the same time (to 16.7 percent) and defied expectations at the 2011 municipal elections (24 percent). It may do even better in 2014. And that's not forgetting that Zille was voted World Mayor of the Year in 2008. So the question is this: is it just coincidence, or can a large part of her success be put down to the fact that she's a woman?

Seriously, in our violent, confrontational, aggressive, machismo land, perhaps what it takes is something of a woman's touch to change perceptions and get people working together. This is not to say that Zille is some kind of feminine vision of maternal goodness; the Godzille is a ball-busting badass who works a 25-hour day and doesn't need a Bar-One to do it. It's just that her X chromosomes seem to be working in her favour.

South Africa (and the ANC) has been strong when it comes to pushing for equal gender representation at governmental level. In Africa there are now three countries with female heads of state: Liberia, Malawi and Senegal. Perhaps it's time for one here. Of course, Helen's dreaming if she thinks it's going to be her. But how about President Mamphela Ramphele or President Thuli Madonsela? Even President Nkosazana Dlamini-Zuma doesn't sound too bad. Whatever happens, though, please god don't let it be President Lulu Xingwana.

[See **Nkosazana Dlamini-Zuma**, **Thuli Madonsela** and **Lulu Xingwana**]

Jacob Zuma

And, finally, we get to the one and only, Jacob Zuma. JZ, Msholozi, Number One, the King of Nkandla, the Big Chief, the Commander in Chief, El-Presidente, the Prez, Mr Turtle Head… Call him what you will, Jacob Gedleyihlekisa Zuma has been analysed from head to toe and editorialised and legally dissected and nitpicked over and pulled apart from every angle, so much so that he must just want the analysers and editors and lawyers and nitpickers to leave him in peace for a moment so he can put his feet up and lose himself in a good book with a cold beer at his side. Except we know that's not going to happen seeing as they say he doesn't read or drink alcohol because that's the type of thing that all the analysing and legalising and editorialising and nitpicking reveals. Even his name has been picked apart to the nth detail; depending on who's doing the picking, Gedleyihlekisa means "one who grinds you while smiling with you" or possibly "one who gangs up against you" or, if you search the comments section on News24 long enough, probably something along the lines of the "one who is very, very naughty and doesn't know what he's doing".

No more picking!

Given that JZ is the most polarising president to walk the earth (clearly), let's simply present a best- and worst-case scenario for the lovers and the haters out there. We can all, I hope, accept that the man's first term as president has been marked by… distractions. Rather than too much actual governing, his first five years in charge seem to have been about entrenching his position at the top: surrounding himself with people he trusts (see **KZN power**), looking out for the individuals who've helped him along the way, not ticking off Cosatu and the SACP too much, dealing with various Guptagate-ish, Nkandla-esque controversies, keeping track of his legal issues, and so on. Which makes actual ruling understandably tricky; these are time-consuming activities, and governing decisions have been few and far between as a result. (For example, it took Zuma eight months to appoint a new head of the National Prosecuting Authority and 18 months to appoint a new head of the Special Investigating Unit.)

So what's the bright side for the JZ lovers out there, who no doubt believe their man is being unnecessarily constrained by all these goings-on around him and want to see him silence the critics? Well, after the 2014 elections, having done what's necessary to retain power, there's a good chance our president may be less distracted by the sideshows and backroom shenanigans and decide to do some presiding. That is, go out there and do stuff. Make decisions. Apply policy. Be presidential. Lead from the front.

And the worst-case scenario for the doubters? Same as above.